——— 🐾 ———

Yesterday is gone.
Tomorrow has not yet come.
We only have today. Let us begin.

—Mother Teresa

——— 🐾 ———

MYSTERIES OF COBBLE HILL FARM

Digging Up Secrets
Hide and Seek
Into Thin Air
Three Dog Knight
Show Stopper
A Little Bird Told Me
The Christmas Camel Caper
On the Right Track
Wolves in Sheep's Clothing
Snake in the Grass
A Will and a Way
Caught in a Trap
Of Bats and Belfries
Stray from the Fold
Borrowed Trouble
Lost at Sea

MYSTERIES OF COBBLE HILL FARM

Lost at Sea

BETH ADAMS

Guideposts

A Gift from Guideposts

Thank you for your purchase! We want to express our gratitude for your support with a special gift just for you.

Dive into *Spirit Lifters*, a complimentary e-book that will fortify your faith, offering solace during challenging moments. Its 31 carefully selected scripture verses will soothe and uplift your soul.

Please use the QR code or go to **guideposts.org/spiritlifters** to download.

Mysteries of Cobble Hill Farm is a trademark of Guideposts.

Published by Guideposts
100 Reserve Road, Suite E200, Danbury, CT 06810
Guideposts.org

Copyright © 2025 by Guideposts. All rights reserved. This book, or parts thereof, may not be reproduced, stored in a retrieval system, or transmitted in any form or by any means, electronic, mechanical, photocopying, recording, or otherwise, without the written permission of the publisher.

This is a work of fiction. While the setting of Mysteries of Cobble Hill Farm as presented in this series is fictional, the location of Yorkshire, England, actually exists, and some places and characters may be based on actual places and people whose identities have been used with permission or fictionalized to protect their privacy. Apart from the actual people, events, and locales that figure into the fiction narrative, all other names, characters, businesses, and events are the creation of the author's imagination and any resemblance to actual persons or events is coincidental. Every attempt has been made to credit the sources of copyrighted material used in this book. If any such acknowledgment has been inadvertently omitted or miscredited, receipt of such information would be appreciated.

Scripture references are from the following sources: *The Holy Bible, King James Version* (KJV). *The Holy Bible, New International Version* (NIV). Copyright ©1973, 1978, 1984, 2011 by Biblica, Inc. Used by permission of Zondervan. All rights reserved worldwide. www.zondervan.com.

Cover and interior design by Müllerhaus
Cover illustration by Bob Kayganich at Illustration Online LLC.
Typeset by Aptara, Inc.

ISBN 978-1-961442-78-8 (hardcover)
ISBN 978-1-961442-79-5 (softcover)
ISBN 978-1-961442-80-1 (epub)

Printed and bound in the United States of America
10 9 8 7 6 5 4 3 2 1

MYSTERIES OF COBBLE HILL FARM

Lost at Sea

GLOSSARY OF UK TERMS

boot • trunk of a car

brekky • breakfast

cheeky • insolent or irreverent, but in an amusing/charming way

footie • soccer

mind • be careful, take care

petrol • gasoline, fuel

posh • fancy, high-class

quid • slang term for British pound

CHAPTER ONE

Harriett Bailey-Knight leaned back against the fiberglass gunwale of the boat and enjoyed the feel of the wind on her cheeks. Behind her, her new husband, Will, and their friend Kyle Manning chatted as Kyle drove his fishing boat north along the coast. Between the roar of the motor and the whipping wind, Harriet couldn't hear what they were talking about, so she decided to just sit back and enjoy the September sunshine.

The day was bright and warm, and Harriet and Will had been happy to accept Kyle's invitation to join him on a fishing excursion after church. Well, Will was happy to join him for the fishing. Harriet was there for the boat ride, and she enjoyed watching the high, craggy cliffs slide past as they made their way back to the Whitby marina. Will's and Kyle's catch—a large cod and several mackerel—were on ice in a cooler, and Harriet looked forward to fresh fish for dinner.

Gazing out toward the coast, eyeing the burnt ocher color of the high cliffs, Harriet tried to make out the buildings of the small towns they passed. She was pretty sure they'd gone past Ravenscar a few minutes ago, which meant...yes, that was White Church Bay. The adorable little fishing village they called home. There was the spillway where generations ago fishermen launched their vessels into the rough seas. There was the hotel and the pub perched on the hill just above them, and she could barely make out the old lifesaving station building. It was high tide now, which meant the water lapped at the spillway and licked at the buildings above. At low tide, the water receded enough that a person could walk out among the rocks for hundreds of yards and treasure hunters seeking jet and fossils could explore the wide, flat bay floor.

As they continued north, Harriet could see more familiar landmarks of their small town—the sea wall, Cliffside Chippy, and, beyond them all, the steeple of White Church. Harriet had only lived in Yorkshire for a year and a half, but it already felt like home.

"Look at that."

It was the first thing Harriet had been able to hear Will say for a while, so he must have said it pretty loudly. She turned to see what he was looking at. He pointed at a sailboat bobbing on the waves. Harriet didn't see what was so interesting about it.

"Where are they?" Will asked.

"Maybe below deck?" Kyle shouted to be heard over the sound of the motor. He grabbed a set of binoculars from inside a compartment near the steering wheel and looked through them at the sailboat. "They're for sure not up top." He handed the binoculars to Will.

Harriet still didn't see what was so intriguing about it. It was a big sailboat, certainly. Probably forty or fifty feet long. The white sails were taut against the stiff wind. It was a nice boat, she could tell that. Expensive, for sure. It dwarfed Kyle's little fishing boat. Whoever was sailing in that thing had money to spare. Below deck, there was probably a nice living area. Which was no doubt where the sailors were right now.

"What's wrong?" Harriet pushed herself up and moved over to the driver's seat so she could hear. "What's with that boat?"

"Maybe nothing," Kyle said, but he turned the steering wheel to change direction, heading toward the sailboat. "It's just that we don't see anyone on deck, and it's unusual to see a boat with its sails unfurled like that with no one around. Something about it looks wrong."

"Wrong how?"

"They're too close to shore, for one thing," Kyle said, raising his voice to be heard over the motor and wind. "We're only a few hundred meters out. If they don't turn soon, they'll be headed right for those rocks."

"Plus, this close to port, they need to look out for other boats and fishing lines," Will said. "And no one seems to be doing that."

"But mostly it's the sails," Kyle said. "Boats like that have motors and use those to get where they want to go most of the time."

"So the sails are just for show?" Harriet asked. As they got closer, she could see that the name *Salacia* was written on the back of the boat in a scripty font.

"No, they'll use the sails, of course." Kyle pushed up the throttle to slow the speed of their boat as it got closer. "When it's feasible. They use the motor in tricky spots or when the winds aren't cooperating."

"But that boat has the sails up and no motor going. It's just floating, so it's at the whim of the winds. Which are currently pushing it toward the rocks at the bottom of that cliff." Will nodded to the shore.

"So we're going to check it out," Harriet said. Of course they were. If someone was in trouble—if someone was sick or hurt, Will would want to help.

"We're going to try the radio first," Kyle said. He lifted the small black handset nest to the steering wheel. "*Salacia*, this is *Seas the Day*, coming toward you on your port side. Do you copy?"

There was no response. Kyle moved a knob to change the channel he was broadcasting over and then tried again. "*Salacia*, this is *Seas the Day*. We're a hundred meters out from you. Do you copy?"

When there was still no answer, Kyle tried a few more channels, but he didn't get a response. Meanwhile, there was no movement on the deck of the sailboat. No evidence that anyone was on board at all.

"Let's put a bulletin out," Will suggested, and Kyle switched the station again.

"This is *Seas the Day*, location just off the coast of White Church Bay, calling the Coastguard. Are there any reports of a sailboat in distress in the vicinity?" Kyle paused, and Harriet strained to hear a response.

At first there was nothing but static, but a moment later, the radio buzzed to life. "*Seas the Day*, there are no reports of a boat in distress," came the reply. "Do you need to make a report?"

"Not yet," Kyle said. "Maybe everything is okay. We'll check it out."

"Keep us posted," said the man at the other end of the line.

Kyle replaced the handset and guided them toward the sailboat. As they got closer, Harriet saw how large the vessel truly was. One of the sails swung back and forth across the deck, moving the giant beam—the boom—that held it up as it swayed. At the rear of the boat was a small sitting area with a steering wheel, but no one sat there.

"Hello?" Kyle called as they neared the ship. "Do you need help?"

Once again, there was no response.

"What do you think?" Will asked. "Should we go on board, just to make sure everything is okay?"

"I don't know." Kyle hesitated, clearly nervous about the idea of going onto someone else's boat without permission. "Hello!" he shouted, louder this time. "Is everything all right?" He pulled an air horn out of the same compartment the binoculars had been in. "This'll wake them up." He pushed the button, and a loud, high-pitched blast sounded. Both Harriet and Will covered their ears, but there was no movement on the sailboat. Kyle sounded the air horn once again, and then another time. They were only a dozen yards or so from the sailboat. Surely anyone on board would have heard that noise.

Then Harriet heard a frantic barking sound, coming from inside the cabin.

"What's that?" Kyle asked.

"It's a dog," Harriet said. "There's a dog on that boat. And it sounds scared."

"The air horn probably freaked it out," Will said. "But if there's anyone human on board, it didn't get their attention."

"We need to see if the dog is okay," Harriet said. "What if its owner is in trouble and it's trying to let us know?"

"You're right, we should check it out, just to be safe," Kyle said reluctantly. Will edged past Kyle to climb, on his hands and knees, onto the front of Kyle's boat. He made his way carefully across the sheet of molded fiberglass that topped the enclosed storage area. While Will grabbed a rope tied to the thin metal railing, Kyle slowly and carefully steered his boat toward the back of the sailboat. When they were close enough that Will could lean over and reach the sailboat, he called out, "Hello! Requesting permission to board your boat!"

Kyle sounded the air horn one more time, and the only response was more frantic barking. Will slipped the rope from Kyle's boat around a railing on the sailboat, and then he pushed himself up and jumped from one boat to the other. Kyle's boat dipped, and Will landed softly on the deck of the sailboat, which barely swayed under his weight.

"My name is Will Knight," Will called out. "I'm a vicar in White Church Bay. I just want to see if you need help."

Again, no sound or movement from inside. As a wave tossed the boat, the boom swung toward Will, whipping the sail around.

"Watch out!" Harriet called. Will ducked just in time.

"Something is definitely not right," Kyle said quietly. "The hatch is wide open."

"I'm going to check inside," Will called out. He started toward the hatch, which Harriet guessed led to a small set of stairs. "Hello," he called again, starting down the steps. "Is anyone here?"

The barking grew more frantic as Will descended, and then went quiet. What had happened? Harriet couldn't begin to guess what Will would find in the cabin, but all signs pointed to it not being good. Were the sailors hurt, or worse? Was there something illegal or dangerous down there? Long moments passed, and Harriet started praying.

And then, when she was starting to get truly scared, Will popped back up above the deck. He climbed the steps, clutching the metal handrail with one hand. In his other arm he cradled a small, brown, shivering Yorkie.

"They're gone," he called out. "There was only the dog."

"What do you mean, they're gone?" Kyle yelled back. "Why would they leave their dog?"

"I have no idea," Will said, coming closer. "It looks like—well, it looks like something happened. Stuff is spilled, and it's a mess inside." He looked dazed, like he was trying to make sense of what he'd seen. "But I can tell you there's definitely no one here. Except for the dog, this boat is sailing with no one on board."

CHAPTER TWO

Kyle got back on the radio immediately after Will's news, and within moments the Coastguard said they were on their way.

"Can you come see if this dog is okay?" Will said to Harriet. "It won't stop shaking."

"The poor thing is probably terrified," Harriet said. Not to mention hungry or thirsty, depending on how long it had been alone on the boat. But Harriet hesitated. Shouldn't they stay off the boat until the authorities got there? If something happened to whoever was supposed to be on board, she didn't want to contaminate a crime scene.

But the little dog did look like it needed help. Shaking like that could mean it was scared, but it could also be a sign of other, more serious problems as well. If it was missing medication it needed, the dog could be in dire straits.

Besides, she was curious. She'd never been on a large sailboat before, and she wondered what it looked like inside, as well as what made Will so sure something had gone wrong.

"I don't think I can jump across like you did," she said. Kyle edged his boat closer, and Will stood near the railing of the sailboat and held out his hand. Harriet crawled across the bow and pushed herself up. There was still a wide strip of dark blue sea between the two boats, but she took Will's hand and jumped onto the deck of the sailboat.

Will loosened his grip on her hand. "You okay?" he asked.

She nodded, and he handed the dog to her. The Yorkie was still shaking, and lighter than she'd expected. She held the little dog against her chest. "You're okay now," she crooned. The dog couldn't understand her words, but it seemed to pick up on her tone, and the shaking eased a bit. The dog wore a pink collar with a bone-shaped name tag attached to it.

"Her name is Mercedes," Harriet said. Unfortunately, there was no phone number or address on the tag. "Is there any food or water here for her?"

"Just a couple of empty dog bowls," Will said. "Come see." He led her to the stairs that went below deck.

She followed him down, clutching Mercedes under one arm, and into what looked like a combined living room and kitchen. There was a table surrounded by banquette seating, and a U-shaped couch that surrounded a small coffee table and backed up against a micro kitchen. Behind her, at the front of the boat, were two small bedrooms and a tiny bathroom. Narrow windows just below the ceiling let in sunlight, as did a skylight, and all the surfaces were finished with polished wood and white canvas.

"It's like a small apartment down here," Harriet said.

"Some people live on boats like this for months or even years at a time," Will said. "This is a nice one. It's not new, but it's well kept."

It did seem really nice. She didn't know how much a boat like this cost, but she imagined that all the chrome and polished wood didn't come cheap. But there was one problem.

"It's kind of a mess," she said. There were glasses and cups scattered on both tables and the kitchen counter, several of which had overturned and spilled their contents onto the floor. Most of the drawers and cabinet doors in the kitchen were open. A sweatshirt and a jacket were draped over the couch, and several pairs of flip-flops and sneakers littered the space in front of it. There were two small metal bowls on the kitchen floor, but both were empty, and water had sloshed out of one of them all over the floor. As much as she wanted to refill the bowls for Mercedes, something told her not to touch anything.

"Exactly," Will said. "It's like they just vanished in the middle of their day." An open laptop sat on the table. "It's weird, right?"

"Totally weird." Harriet leaned over the laptop. It looked as if someone had been checking their email and was called away for some reason and never came back. She stepped around the staircase to the front of the boat, where the two small bedrooms branched off the short hallway. Both rooms were barely big enough to hold a double bed and not much else. Judging by the clothing she saw, one of the rooms was occupied by both a man and a woman, and it looked, again, as if they were in the middle of dressing for their day when something called them away.

"Besides checking out the dog, I wanted you to take a look, to see if there's some obvious clue about where they are that I missed," Will said.

Harriet looked inside the tiny bathroom, which held a toilet, a small sink, and a stand-up shower. A tube of lipstick sat on the edge of the sink. Harriet shook her head. "Is there any other place they could go?"

"There's got to be a mechanical room here somewhere," Will said. "But I'm not sure where that would be." Harriet wandered back into the kitchen area and saw a brown leather journal sitting on the counter, between the dirty glasses. *Captain's Log* was written in black marker across the cover. She pulled her sleeve over her hand, opened the book, and skimmed a few pages. Someone had written entries in blue ink nearly every day starting in June.

June 12. 12:30 p.m. Cloudy again today, and cool, but beautiful scenery sailing around the western tip.

June 15. 4:30 p.m. Storm coming tomorrow, so we'll stay in port another day. I can't complain about having another day to explore Cardiff.

July 5. 6:00 p.m. Sunshine and a beautiful northern wind meant we got to Aberystwyth sooner than expected today. Nice port, though the harbor is tricky to get into. Took a walk through the national park after lunch. This is what sailing is all about.

Harriet turned a few pages and saw that they'd recorded the weather and stops at Liverpool, Blackpool, and the Lake District before venturing farther north into Scotland during the long summer days and then back down the east coast of England.
"Are they sailing around the UK?" she asked.
"Maybe," Will said. "It's totally possible. It's a thing people do, and this is the kind of boat you'd do it in."
Harriet flipped forward to the most recent entries, where someone had recorded stops in Craster, Amble, Blyth, Tynemouth, and Sunderland, as well as a few entries from days at sea.

September 12. 8:30 p.m. Another beautiful day in Sunderland, nice walk along the coast, and beautiful beaches. We'll stay here one more night and then set sail again tomorrow.

It was Sunday, and this entry was dated two days ago. If they set sail from Sunderland yesterday, how long had this boat been floating? Sunderland was only about sixty miles from White Church Bay by car. How fast would a boat cover that distance tracing the coast? What had happened between Sunderland and here?

The last entry was dated September 13, at 10 p.m.

Storm came up suddenly. Paul is on deck tying down the sails, but we're really getting tossed around, so I want to record what's happening, just in case. Big black clouds, lightning, we're getting pummeled. I've nearly been swept off the deck several times by the waves. It looks bad. I'd better get back out there.

"Will, look at this," Harriet said. She gestured at the book. "It's a log where they recorded weather and stuff about their journey. It says they were hit by a storm last night, and it was bad. That was the last entry."

"Oh dear," Will said. He walked over to take a look. He read the entry and said, "It doesn't sound good. Let's hope they're okay." He cocked his head. "I'd heard there was going to be a storm last night, north of here. I guess that's the weather they ran into."

They looked around one last time, searching for any hidden cupboard or room they hadn't yet found where the couple might be hiding, but there was no one on board. They headed back up the stairs and out onto the deck, Mercedes still tucked under Harriet's arm. She heard the whine of boat motors heading toward them and saw a red and white boat race through the waves and slow as it neared the spot where Kyle's boat and the sailboat were tied together. Harriet and Will stood on the deck of the *Salacia* while His Majesty's Coastguard boat approached.

They watched as the boat slowed and a man in a blue jumpsuit and a fluorescent yellow jacket jumped nimbly onto the deck of the sailboat.

"Hello, Will," he said as he found his balance. His accent was Scottish, and though Will would probably be able to pick out what part of Scotland, she was proud of herself for having gotten that much. "Mrs. Knight."

"Good to see you, Eli," Will said.

Harriet smiled and added, "Nice to see you." In truth, she had no idea who he was, but she'd already learned that part of being a minister's wife was greeting everyone warmly, as if she knew exactly who they were. Had she met Eli before? She didn't remember seeing him at church.

A young officer in a yellow jacket followed Eli onto the deck of the *Salacia* and greeted them, introducing herself as Officer Vasquez. Two more officers waited on the Coastguard boat.

"We saw this boat floating on the waves, with its sails up, but no one on deck," Will explained. "We came closer to see if anyone needed help."

"We received your message inquiring about whether there had been any distress calls," Officer Vasquez said. "And heard you hailing the boat on the other channels. You never received an answer?"

"We did not," Will said. "But we were worried something was really wrong. It just seemed so odd floating like that, the boom swaying from side to side, with no one around."

"Right you are," Eli said. "That does seem very strange."

"And then we heard a dog barking, so we boarded the boat to check it out," Will said. "The dog was there alone. There's no sign of anyone on board."

"And there's a big mess inside," Harriet added. "It looks like they left all of a sudden."

Officer Vasquez nodded at Eli. "We'd better go check it out. You two can head back to your own boat. But stick around in case we have more questions."

"Can I take Mercedes with me?" Harriet asked. At their blank looks, she added, "That's the dog's name. She was really scared at first, but she seems to have calmed down some since I've been holding her."

"Right. Okay," Eli said.

Harriet handed the dog to Will while Kyle helped her climb back into his boat. Will followed behind and returned the dog to Harriet, who scrambled across the bow to the deck. Will stayed perched at the front of the boat. The two Coastguard officers disappeared into the lower part of the sailboat.

"Could you hand me a water bottle?" Harriet asked Kyle. He reached into the storage compartment under the bow, grabbed one of the water bottles there, and held it out for Harriet. She set Mercedes down, unscrewed the top of the bottle, cupped one hand, and poured water into it. The little dog lapped quickly, and Harriet kept pouring water into her hand until Mercedes stopped drinking.

The two officers emerged from below the sailboat's deck a few minutes later.

"Right," Eli called out. "We don't know what's going on, but clearly there's no one on board and something happened to the sailors. We're going to secure the sails and tow the boat back to the Whitby marina."

"Will you start a search for the missing sailors?" Harriet asked.

"Yes," Eli said. "We'll have the police take a look at the boat and see if there's anything that helps explain what happened. In the meantime, we'll send out several boats and a helicopter to search the area for any sign of them."

"It said in their logbook that they were in a storm last night," Harriet said.

"That was a pretty rough storm," Eli said. "Didn't really affect land very much, but if they were out in the water, it could have been nasty."

"We saw the entry too," Officer Vasquez said. "Because of the storm, we're working with the assumption that they're lost at sea—"

Even though Harriet had come to the same conclusion herself, it was still shocking to hear it from the Coastguard officer, and beside her, she saw Will cringe.

"—and we're going to do everything we can to find them," she continued quickly. "We'll put out a message to all the boats in the area to keep an eye out. Good work calling this in. Hopefully we're not too late and they're in the area somewhere. If they are, we'll find them."

"We'll be praying that you do," Will said.

Eli sent a grateful look his way then said, "You all can head back in if you want."

"What about the dog?" Will asked. "What should we do with her?"

Eli looked at Harriet. "Do you mind holding on to her for now?" he asked. "I don't know what we'd do with her at the station, and I can't think of anyone better to keep her."

"Of course." Harriet had been hoping he would say that.

"Thank you for your quick response," Kyle said to the officers as Will bent over to untie the rope between the two boats. Once Will was safely back on deck, Kyle slowly motored away from the sailboat. Harriet watched as the officers expertly took in the *Salacia*'s sails.

"Well, what do you think?" Kyle asked. "Should we head home?"

"Maybe we could spend some time looking around, just to see if we spot anything, before we head back," Will suggested.

"You okay with that, Harriet?" Kyle asked.

"Please." As anxious as she was to get some food into the little pup, Harriet couldn't imagine returning to the marina now, not when they knew the sailors could be out there somewhere needing help. She picked Mercedes up and held her close.

"All right," Kyle said, and eased the boat to a higher speed. "The question is, where to look?"

"They've been traveling south down the coast, and their last stop was Sunderland," Harriet said. "Their logbook said they were going to leave there yesterday."

"If that's the case, they could be anywhere by now," Kyle said. "The current could have swept them out to sea in that time."

"Let's hope it didn't," Will said. "Let's pray they're still not too far from the coast."

"Is there any hope of finding them?" Harriet didn't want to be a downer, but she also wanted to know if they were embarking on a fool's errand. If the sailors had been swept overboard last night, how long could they survive in the open sea?

"Of course there's hope," Kyle said. "Was the life raft still on board? Or life jackets?"

"I actually didn't think to look," Will said. "Which seems short-sighted now."

"It's not. Why would you look? You were trying to find the people. But the Coastguard will look, for sure. And if the sailors are on a life raft, they have a pretty decent shot."

"Do we know the sailboat had a life raft on board?" Harriet asked. "Is that a thing boats like that have?"

"We don't know for sure. They're not required. But on a boat that size it would be foolish not to have one," Will said.

But if they'd been swept overboard in a storm, how would they have had time or the wherewithal to grab a life raft?

"And even if they didn't have a life raft, it's possible they were able to find something else to cling to," Kyle said. "I remember seeing a video of a guy being rescued by the US Coast Guard after a hurricane in Florida a couple years back. He'd been swept off his boat and was found the next day floating on a cooler."

"A cooler?"

"A heavy-duty cooler, but still. So if they're in a life raft, there's a good chance they could be found safe and sound," Kyle said.

"As long as they're found soon," Will added.

Kyle pulled down on the throttle, and the motor raced. He pointed the boat away from the coastline, and they sped out into the North Sea. Harriet scanned the horizon, looking for...well, she didn't know what exactly. People, she supposed. Hopefully some kind of life raft. What would it look like? Harriet had been on a cruise once, many years ago, to celebrate her parents' anniversary. The cruise left from Boston and stopped in Maine as well as several places in Canada, including Prince Edward Island, where they'd toured L.M. Montgomery's Green Gables. Looking back now, Harriet could see how special that trip had been, though at the time she'd wished the cruise was to the Caribbean or Disney's private island. She remembered strolling around the deck with her grandfather, looking for whales, and seeing the enormous lifeboats that hung from the ceiling. It wouldn't be hard to spot a big orange boat against the dark water, but of course, any life raft that would fit on the *Salacia* had to be a lot smaller than those.

"The RNLI is launching from White Church Bay," Kyle called out over the sound of the engine. Harriet was glad to hear that. The RNLI—The Royal National Lifeboat Institution—was an old organization. Their job was to rescue sailors in trouble, and though that usually meant racing to help when a boat was in distress on the sea, the current situation definitely fit the brief. The more boats out there searching for the missing sailors, the better.

Kyle went away from the coast for quite a while and then turned north. "The current typically heads this way," he said by way of explanation. Way out there, the water was smooth, and there were fewer boats, mostly large fishing vessels and one whale-watching tour. Harriet searched the horizon, looking for anything that might be the missing boaters. They passed colorful buoys marking the location of lobster traps, but there wasn't anything that looked like a life raft. The low-pitched whirring of a helicopter's rotors sounded in the distance, and Harriet watched as it flew toward them. As it passed overhead, Harriet saw that the copter had the distinctive red and white markings of His Majesty's Coastguard.

"We'd better turn around," Kyle said. "It's getting late, and we'll need to get fuel soon. We have enough to make it home, but we can't keep going out much farther."

Harriet hadn't noticed how low in the sky the sun had sunk. She focused on the water around them as Kyle turned the boat and headed back to shore. She kept searching, looking for any sign of the missing sailors, but as they neared the Whitby marina, she felt her hope evaporating. As they rounded the headland where the ghostly remains of Whitby Abbey stood, perched high on the cliff overlooking the town, she reminded herself that there were other people still out there searching. And God knew where the missing sailors were.

Kyle slowed his boat as they entered the narrow marina. Whitby was a beautiful old town, built along the hills that sloped on both sides of the harbor. On this sunny September Sunday, visitors strolled its bridges and alongside the shops and restaurants that fronted the marina. Their boat passed the commercial piers, where the professional fishing boats docked, and then the sightseeing boats that offered whale watching and pirate tours and many others designed to part tourists from their money. Beyond that were the docks where ordinary citizens moored their boats, if they were lucky enough to have secured a boat slip. Kyle pulled up at the slip he'd inherited from his grandfather and tied up his boat.

"Well, that wasn't exactly the calm, relaxing afternoon I promised you," Kyle said as he began to wipe down the inside of the boat with a towel.

"We caught plenty of fish," Will said. "And I'm glad we came across that boat when we did."

"Yeah, it wouldn't have fared well against those cliffs," Kyle said. "It's a lucky thing we found it."

"Now let's just hope they find the people who were on board," Harriet said.

"We can do more than hope," Will said. "We can pray." He reached out and took Harriet's hand, and she realized that he meant to pray right there. She took his hand gratefully.

Kyle set the towel down and bowed his head, and Will asked God to direct the rescuers along the right path so they would find the missing boaters quickly. He asked the Lord to protect the sailors, wherever they were, and that they would be kept from all harm.

As Will said amen, Harriet felt her heart lighten. The Lord was bigger than any sea. He was the one who set the sea in its place to begin with, and who kept the oceans in their boundaries. She didn't know where the missing sailors were, but God did.

Once the boat was cleaned and locked up, Harriet and Will followed Kyle down the long floating dock to the shore. Harriet didn't have a leash handy, so she kept Mercedes tucked under her arm. Will carried a plastic cooler with the fish, and Kyle held a bucket that had contained bait. Even though the day hadn't gone as planned, it had felt nice to be out on the water on such a beautiful afternoon.

As they walked down the dock, Mercedes began to bark again, sharp and insistent. "It's okay, sweet puppy," Harriet said soothingly, but her words seemed to only make the dog more agitated. She yapped and scrambled to get out of Harriet's arms, but Harriet held on tight. Mercedes's barks grew softer, but more forlorn, as they neared the end of the dock.

"I wonder if she knows they're out there somewhere and is upset about leaving the water," Will said.

"Maybe." Harriet knew better than to speculate about what was going on inside an animal's mind. There was no way to know, really. They walked through the locked gate that kept the public off the private docks and were headed for the parking lot when Harriet recognized a familiar face coming toward them.

"Hello, Shane," Kyle called out.

Shane O'Grady was well known around the marina. He had something of a sordid past—there was a reason he was known to most as Shady O'Grady—but he'd turned over a new leaf and a few months ago had even helped chase down a man who was trying to smuggle historical artifacts out of the country. He'd actually been to church a few times over the past few months. Shane O'Grady was proof that people could change.

"Afternoon." Shane ducked his head as he approached, carrying two big bags of fast-food chicken. "Did you have a nice time on the water?"

"It was beautiful out there," Will said. "Though we had some excitement, to say the least."

"Oh yeah?" Shane cocked his head. "What happened?"

"We found a sailboat floating on the water with no one on board," Kyle said. "A big one."

"No one except this precious thing," Harriet said, stroking Mercedes's head. It seemed to calm the dog some.

"That's odd," Shane said. "So no one was sailing the boat?"

"The Coastguard came out. They think the sailors might have been washed overboard," Will said.

"Yikes," Shane said. "That's terrible."

"They're calling for all boats in the area to look out for them," Will continued.

"If you're headed out soon, maybe keep an eye out," Kyle said.

"Sadly, I don't think I'm going out anytime soon. My fuel line gave out yesterday, and the store in town doesn't have the right part in stock. It's maddening to be stuck at the dock on a day like today."

"I'm sorry to hear that," Kyle said. "Can't go anywhere until you get that fixed."

"Tell me about it," Shane said. "Last thing I need after what happened with my mom's house. It feels like I'm bleeding money."

Harriet had been praying for Marsha O'Grady since a grease fire had taken out her kitchen a few weeks ago. Shane was talking to the insurance company and trying to help her get her kitchen repaired, and Will was really pleased when Shane had asked for her name to be added to the prayer list at church.

"Anyway, I decided to make the best of it and do some upkeep on the rest of the boat. I've been tinkering all day." He held up the bags with the familiar logo of the chicken restaurant. "I decided to take a break to refuel before I get back at it. But if I do get it going again, I'll keep an eye out."

"Good luck," Will called, and Shane sauntered to the slip where his fishing boat was tied up. His boat was much bigger than Kyle's, with more space in the hull and an added raised steering area. Various fishing poles and rods hung from different parts of the top level.

"That chicken smelled so good," Will said, and Harriet laughed.

"I didn't want to be the one to say it, but now I really want fried chicken for dinner," she said.

"Just think about how good this fish is going to taste. Fresh from the sea like this?" Kyle shrugged. "Fried chicken can't even compare."

He was right. Plus, Will had promised to descale and fillet the fish, so she wouldn't have to handle any of the gross parts of cooking fresh fish.

"Thank you for a fun afternoon," Will said when they reached the cars. "And for providing our dinner."

"Thank you for joining me. Fishing's always more fun when you're not doing it alone," Kyle said. "You two have a good night. And keep me posted on what you hear about those boaters."

"We will. And if you hear anything, please let us know too," Harriet said.

Kyle promised he would, and Harriet got into Will's car and settled Mercedes in her lap. As they rode along the country roads that wound through fields of heather and rapeseed dotted with woolly sheep, Will started to hum.

"What tune is that?" Harriet asked. She'd heard the song before but couldn't place it.

"'Eternal Father, Strong to Save,'" Will said. "The Royal Navy Hymn. Though, actually, I think the American Navy claims it as well. You know it:

"Eternal Father, strong to save,
Whose arm hath bound the restless wave,
Who bidd'st the mighty ocean deep

Its own appointed limits keep;
Oh hear us when we cry to thee,
For those in peril on the sea."

As Will sang the lyrics in his strong baritone, Harriet realized she did know the song. The pastor at the church where she'd grown up liked to sing the old hymn, though the town where she'd lived in Connecticut was decidedly inland.

"It's popular here, since fishing and shipping are so much a part of our history," Will said. "It was playing in my head, thinking about whatever happened to those sailors."

"The Lord hears us," Harriet said. "Let's hope they'll be found soon."

"Amen to that." Will kept humming the tune as he drove the rest of the way home.

CHAPTER THREE

Will not only cleaned and scaled the fish, he insisted on cooking them himself with a recipe he'd found online. He didn't have a lot of experience, but he'd been eager to try his hand at cooking ever since they'd gotten back from their honeymoon a few weeks ago.

"Are you sure?" Harriet eyed the recipe and saw that it called for breading and frying the fish, which could be tricky. And while his attempts at cooking had so far been...well, interesting, Harriet was happy for him to learn. Her mother did all the cooking for the family when Harriet was growing up, and Harriet was happy to share the load in her own marriage.

"I've got this." Will waved her away. "Why don't you go put your feet up."

"Thank you." She leaned in and kissed him and then poured a small bowl of water for Mercedes and set out some food. Maxwell ran over and sniffed the newcomer, but Mercedes was only interested in the food. She quickly devoured what was in the bowl, and Harriet refilled it. Once the little dog had eaten her fill, Harriet went over to the clinic and got a spare doggy bed and set it next to Maxwell's. The little dachshund sniffed Mercedes, but Mercedes wagged her tail and settled down on the bed, so Maxwell went and stood by the back door until Harriet let him out.

Once the dogs were happy, Harriet headed to the small nook where the washer and dryer were hidden. She couldn't fault Will for his intentions, though there was no way she could go and put her feet up. She emptied the dryer and carried the laundry basket to the bedroom. Will's cat, Ash Wednesday, looked up from Will's side of the bed.

"Still in here, Ash?"

The kitten watched her for a minute and then hissed at her. He'd liked her just fine while she and Will were dating, but not so much since the wedding. Will thought Ash was still adjusting to his new home and having to share it with Maxwell and Charlie, Harriet's cat. Charlie had hissed at Ash the first time he tried to eat out of her food dish, and the sound of the wheels on Maxwell's prosthesis obviously freaked Ash out. So far, he'd been giving both animals a wide berth. Harriet knew change was hard for cats, but she also knew that wasn't the real problem.

It wasn't his new life or the other animals Ash struggled with. It was Harriet.

Before Harriet and Will were married, Will had totally spoiled Ash, petting him practically nonstop and even letting the little cat sleep with him. Now, Ash had to share Will with Harriet, and Ash did not like it. It sounded ridiculous to say that the cat was jealous of Harriet, but she'd seen it plenty of times before. Oh, well. Harriet would just keep showing him affection, and hopefully she'd win him over in the end.

For now, Harriet decided to use the other side of the bed to fold the clean laundry. She started making piles of clothing, carefully avoiding Ash's side of the bed, and as she did the repetitive task, her mind kept going to those missing sailors. What happened to them?

Were they swept overboard in the storm? If that was the case, Harriet was afraid there wasn't much hope for them. How long could a person tread water? Would they succumb to the cold before their arms and legs gave out? What about if they were on a life raft? They would fare better in that situation. They would need fresh water, most importantly, and food, but they might make it several days. They might be okay, if they had—

She was startled from her thoughts by a loud bleating sound. The smoke alarm. Ash jumped off the bed and scrambled underneath it. Harriet rushed downstairs and into the kitchen, to find Will waving a towel at the smoke detector. Mercedes howled from her bed, obviously disturbed by the noise.

"Sorry!" Will said cheerfully. "Looks like things got a little smoky in here."

"Looks like it." It was more than a little smoky. A thick gray cloud hung in the air. She rushed to open windows and doors and then turned on the air vent over the stove. The alarm continued to bleat every few seconds. Charlie had vanished, scared by the noise. After a few more minutes of Will waving the towel, the alarm finally fell silent.

"Good news," Will said with a grin. "The smoke alarm works!"

"Now we know there's not much chance of sleeping through that," Harriet said. "What happened?"

"I think I let the oil get a little too hot," Will said with a shrug. "I'll keep it lower this time."

"But you need it hot to fry the fish, don't you?" Harriet walked to the stove to take a look. A glistening skin of oil coated the bottom of the pan beneath the breaded fish, still sending up tendrils of smoke. Harriet glanced at the bottle of oil on the counter. Extra virgin olive oil. "Did you use this?"

"Yeah, because you love olive oil."

It was true, she was a fan of olive oil in dips and on salads. But it wasn't used for frying, because it would smoke, as Will had just proved.

"I do, but vegetable oil is better for frying. It has a higher smoke point."

"Huh. Well, I've learned something new today," Will said. "Sorry about that."

"It's okay," Harriet said. "How would you have known that unless someone told you?"

Part of Harriet didn't quite understand how someone got to be a thirty-five-year-old living on their own without learning to cook beyond the basics, but then she remembered that members of the congregation—often, single women—had made Will meals so often that he hadn't needed to cook much for himself. It was sweet that he wanted to learn, that he wanted to share the responsibilities of their new home equally. It would just take him some time to get up to speed.

"Let's get this smoke cleared out, and then you can switch pans and try it again with vegetable oil." She took the dish towel from Will and used it to wave the smoke out the door as best she could, and a few minutes later, once the air was clearer, she pulled out another pan and the vegetable oil. Will may not be a top chef yet, but he was great in all the ways that mattered.

As Will worked on frying the fish again, Harriet went to check on Ash, who was still hiding under the bed. She tried to coax him out, but he hissed at her. She admitted defeat and returned to the kitchen where Will was plating the fish.

"It got a little done," he said, gesturing at the charred breading. "But I think it's still going to be delicious."

It was more than a little done. It was burned. But Will looked so proud of himself that Harriet couldn't help but smile. She hadn't married him for his cooking, after all. She couldn't be happier to be married to Will and to be finally spending day and night together. She loved that he wanted to do his part with the cooking and the cleaning. But that didn't mean things would always go smoothly. It would, she thought again, just take some time.

CHAPTER FOUR

Will still slept, his arms splayed out, when Harriet crept out of bed on Monday morning. Ash, who was curled up against him, glared at her as she grabbed her clothes and tiptoed to the door. Harriet had never allowed her pets to sleep in bed with her, but she hadn't yet been able to convince either Will or the kitten to give up the habit. Will was afraid Ash wouldn't be able to sleep without him. Harriet didn't have the heart to remind him that cats are nocturnal. There were worse things her husband could bring into their marriage than a soft spot for a fluffy kitten. Even a fluffy kitten who wanted her out of the picture.

Harriet closed the bedroom door softly. Will's first meeting wasn't until ten, so he would sleep in for at least another hour, but Harriet had an early morning appointment to give vaccinations to a herd of alpacas, and she needed to get going. She dressed in the bathroom, pulling on a warm wool sweater over her flannel shirt. Even though it was only September, mornings could be chilly, so she put on wool socks as well before washing her face, brushing her teeth, and pulling her hair into a low ponytail. Then she went down to the kitchen and started the coffee.

Charlie stood up and stretched from her position on the couch. She sauntered over, looking for her breakfast, and Harriet tossed some food in her bowl before hooking up Maxwell's harness and letting him and Mercedes out into the yard. Maxwell brought a stick over to Mercedes, and Harriet knew he was trying to engage the Yorkie in keep-away, his favorite game, but Mercedes didn't seem to want to play. Hopefully, the little dog would get used to her new surroundings before too long. No, hopefully they would find Mercedes's owners soon and return her to them.

Once the dogs were back inside and eating their breakfast, Harriet made an egg and a piece of toast for herself. She sat down at the table with her breakfast and opened her Bible to her daily reading. It was the passage in Matthew about Jesus calming the storm. *Well, that's well-timed*, Harriet thought as she read the story of how Jesus fell asleep in the boat and the disciples, afraid of the storm, woke Him up. Jesus, unconcerned, told the waves to be still, and they obeyed.

Too bad Jesus wasn't in the boat with those missing sailors, Harriet thought. Then she corrected herself, because of course He had been! She prayed the Lord would help them, wherever they were. Then Harriet pushed herself up, loaded her plate and mug into the dishwasher, and started toward the door.

But then she stopped and went back to the kitchen. She reached for the teakettle, refilled it, and set it on the stove so it would be ready to go when Will got up, and then she pulled out a tea bag and set it in his favorite mug. She may never understand how someone could drink tea instead of coffee first thing in the morning, but that didn't mean she couldn't make it easy for him.

She grabbed her vet bag and loaded it into the Beast—her affectionate name for the vintage Land Rover she'd inherited, along with the house and the vet practice, from her grandfather, and set off.

The country roads that wound through the gentle hills of Yorkshire were beautiful at any time of day, but the morning fog was gathered in the hollows, and the landscape had an almost ethereal quality to it. She traced the coast then turned inland a few miles north of White Church Bay, and easily found the dirt road that led to the Baker farm, tucked away in a beautiful valley. Harriet pulled into the driveway and parked in front of the barn. She could see that the alpacas were already gathered in the pen to the left of the barn. She stepped out of the car, grabbed her bag, and started toward them. The Bakers sold the alpaca wool to yarn processors in the area, who cleaned and dyed and spun it into costly skeins that were sold in a knitting shop in the village. It took a lot to go from animal in the field to sweater, and that was reflected in the price.

"Good morning, Rupert," Harriet called to the man standing by the fence. He had gray hair under a tweed flat cap and wore a heavy canvas jacket.

Rupert waved and called back, "Morning, Harriet. Thank you for coming."

"Of course." Harriet walked over to the split-rail fence and reached out her hand to a camel-colored alpaca. "These guys look like they're doing well." Three new crias—the name for baby alpacas—had joined the herd last spring, and they seemed to be growing up just fine.

"Right as rain," Rupert said, nodding. "Mind the mud." He opened a gate and led her into the paddock area, and Harriet checked the young alpacas over. Then she began administering the yearly vaccinations to the rest of the animals. As she worked her way through the herd, she realized she had a visitor coming her way.

"Who's this guy?" she said, gesturing at a giant tortoise that was slowly making its way across the pen.

"Ah, that's old Jim," Rupert said. "He must think you're here to give him his brekky."

"Aren't you a pretty one." Harriet stepped away from the alpacas and turned to the tortoise. She'd always been fascinated by them. Unlike aquatic turtles, giant tortoises were land animals and could grow to be quite large. This guy was at least four feet long and probably three feet high, with a thick shell and scaly skin on his face and legs. A Seychelles giant tortoise, if she guessed correctly.

"I would have named him Sheldon, if it had been up to me," Rupert said.

"You didn't name him?"

"Oh, no. This guy has been around far longer than I have. You see those markings on his shell? They were there when my great-grandfather got him."

Harriet moved toward the tortoise and looked closer. There were faint initials carved into the keratin of Jim's shell. "I suppose I should have guessed his name," she said. She didn't like seeing that. It wasn't comfortable for the animal, though the carving would inflict no long-lasting pain if not done too deeply. She was glad to see that was the case with Jim.

"This was your great-grandfather's tortoise?" Harriet asked. She knew that tortoises could live a very long time. But it still felt crazy to think that one right in front of her was that old.

"Sure was. He's been passed down through the generations, along with the farm. Old Jim is the most constant thing we have around here."

"Do you know how old he is?" It was nearly impossible to make an accurate judgment about a tortoise's age based on its appearance, but now that she looked more closely, she could see that Jim had a smooth shell, which could indicate an older animal.

"No clue. I know he was around when my grandfather was born, and that was in 1899. I'm not sure how long his father had him before that."

"Blimey." The Britishism felt like the only appropriate response. So the tortoise was at least a hundred and twentysomething years old. This guy was older than the Model T Ford. Older than the Titanic. He could have been around as long ago as the beginning of the Civil War.

"Yep. It's nice to know I'm not the oldest thing on this farm," Rupert said with a laugh. Harriet smiled. Rupert was only in his early seventies, she guessed. This tortoise could be double that.

"You have no idea who carved those letters, or when?"

"None," Rupert said. "As long as he's been here, he's been Jim."

Harriet looked over the tortoise's shell again, narrowing in on the letters carved into it. There was a *J*, and what looked like an *M*. The *I* actually looked more like it was a part of the coloration of the shell than an actual carving. But it was hard to tell.

"Jim seems to be doing just fine, especially considering his age," she said.

"I'm glad to hear it," Rupert said. "Jim is like a member of the family."

"Could I take a few pictures?" Polly would want to see him.

"Of course."

Harriet pulled out her phone and took a few photographs. She wished Rupert well and headed back to the clinic, still marveling over the surprise of finding a giant tortoise in Yorkshire—and one that was so old, at that! The species was from the Seychelles, off the east coast of Africa, north of Madagascar, and was considered critically endangered because of overharvesting. How had this one come to live in the Yorkshire countryside so long ago?

When Harriet pulled into the lot outside the clinic, she saw that Will's car was still parked in front of the house. Maybe she'd pop in and say hello before heading over to see her first patient of the day. She walked inside and found Will seated at the table with his Bible open in front of him, sipping a cup of tea.

"Well, hello," he said, smiling. He had a small plate in front of him dotted with crumbs from a piece of toast.

"Good morning, sleepyhead." She bent to kiss him. "Did you sleep all right?"

"Just great, until Eli called."

"Who's Eli?" Harriet knew she'd heard the name recently, but she couldn't place it.

"Eli Baine. From the Coastguard. He was one of the officers who responded to the call yesterday."

"Why haven't I met him before?" Harriet asked.

"You have." Will laughed. "He was at our wedding."

"Oh." While the reception after their wedding was for a small group of invited guests, the ceremony itself had been open to the public—as the minister of the local church, Will had felt like it needed to be—and Harriet shook hundreds of hands that day. Eli must have been among them, though she had no recollection of meeting him. The whole day was something of a blur, and she had been distracted looking for a brooch that went missing. "Why did he call you this morning?"

"He called to let us know they had to stop the search last night when it got dark but that they're going out again this morning. They've put out a notice to all boats in the area to keep an eye out for the missing sailors."

"I was hoping we'd have better news."

Will took her hand. "We'll just keep praying," he said.

Harriet kissed him goodbye and then opened the door that led from her kitchen to the clinic. She ushered Charlie and Maxwell through—Ash wasn't interested in joining the fun, and she thought Mercedes was already dealing with enough change—and then followed the two furballs down the hallway to the waiting room. Polly was already at her desk, sipping a cup of tea.

"Hey," Harriet said. "How's it going?"

"You were there when they found that boat, right?"

"Uh, yes?" Harriet said. "You know about it?"

"Know about it? I'm obsessed. Last night Van got home late because he had to investigate a sailboat found with no one on board, and I was kind of put out at first, honestly, because I'd made this lamb tagine that I know he likes, and I'd spent hours working on it, right? But when he told me the name of the sailboat, I knew immediately who was missing."

"You did?" A couple of months back, Polly had married Van Worthington, a detective constable on the local police force. Eli had said they were going to have the police check out the boat after they towed it to the marina, and Van must have been part of the team that scoured it looking for clues about the sailors' disappearance. So that part made sense. It was the other part that didn't.

"What do you mean, you know who it was?" she asked.

"Van told me the sailboat was the *Salacia*, and I recognized the name right away. That's Annie and Paul Bellingham. They're social media influencers. I'm obsessed with their channel."

"They're social media influencers?"

"Have you really never heard of them? You must be, like, the only person in the UK who doesn't follow them. Come see."

Harriet saw that Polly already had a social media channel pulled up on her computer. She must have been looking at it before Harriet came in.

"They used to post about their life in London. They're quite posh, and they went to fancy parties and took elaborate trips to places like Morocco and Egypt. But last spring they announced they were giving up their London life and were going to spend the summer and early fall sailing around the UK, and that's when their channel really took off. The subscriber count has quadrupled, at least. Which, I mean, it makes sense, right, because who doesn't dream of doing something like that? Just chucking it all and seeing the world? What an amazing life, you know?"

"These are their videos?" Harriet saw a bunch of recordings on the home page.

"Yeah. See, here's them talking about their boat." Polly clicked on the video at the top of the page, and when it started playing after a short ad, Harriet saw a woman with stylish clothes, perfectly highlighted hair, and artistically applied makeup gesturing excitedly at a huge sailboat.

"This is the one!" the woman said in the video. "I've dreamed and schemed and saved and worked for this for so long, and I can't believe it's finally coming true!"

As the camera panned around the boat, Harriet saw the name *Salacia* on the back. It was written in script, just as it had been on the boat she'd seen yesterday.

"She couldn't have needed to save and work for that long," Polly said. "She's got a huge trust fund. I think she says stuff like that to make herself seem relatable, but I don't even care. They're so cool, and their trip has been so interesting to follow."

"They've been making videos about their trip?"

"Yeah, for the last few months that's all they've been posting about. They started in Plymouth and went up the west coast, stopping in Wales and then on up to Scotland, and now they're making it back down the east side."

"It sounds like quite a trip," Harriet said. "And they just post videos about the places where they stop?"

"Well, that's how their videos started off, anyway. They get more interesting as they go along."

"What do you mean?"

"At first, they were making videos about the places where they stopped. Not only the big tourist places, where they wined and dined like royalty, but little villages the average person will probably never go to."

As Polly said it, Harriet realized how appealing that was. People liked those videos because they wanted to be Annie and Paul, or at least, be *like* them.

"But about a month ago, things started going wrong, and that's when they started to pick up more followers."

"Is there anything on their page about what happened to them recently?" Harriet asked.

"No, that's what I looked for this morning," Polly said. "I checked to see if they'd posted anything about whatever happened, but there's nothing. Their most recent video was from last week, when they were in Sunderland."

Harriet squinted at the screen as Polly pointed at the latest video. The still image showed two beautiful young people, hand in hand, walking down a narrow cobbled street lined with shops and cafés. "Can I see?"

Just then, the door opened, and Earl Soddelmeier walked in, carrying his mixed-breed dog, Naughty.

"I guess it'll have to be later," Harriet said, straightening up. "Hi, Earl."

"Hi, Harriet. Thanks so much for seeing us this morning." Earl rubbed his dog's ears. "Naughty's been sick since last night. I'm sure he just ate something he shouldn't have, but I wanted to get it checked out."

"Let's go take a look," Harriet said. She led them down the hall and into an exam room. She did her best to focus on the dog, who, she was pretty sure, had indeed eaten something strange—and with a dog, it truly could be anything—but even as she wrote a prescription for an anti-emetic medication, her mind was on the missing sailors. She thought about them while she gave a kitten its vaccinations, while she did a checkup on a dog who had been spayed two weeks ago, and while she treated a potbellied pig with a gastric ulcer.

When they finally had a break for lunch, Polly called to Harriet, "You want to see more of those videos?"

"I hate to admit how much I do," she called back.

"Go on, grab your lunch, and I'll show you."

Harriet went into the house and made a sandwich and then brought it back to the clinic. Polly had pulled a chair behind her workstation, and Harriet sat down. Polly pushed the play button on one of the videos.

"Hi, I'm Annie—"

"And I'm Paul—"

"And in this channel, you see into our lives and our world," Annie said. She was probably in her late twenties, Harriet guessed, and had brown hair with caramel-colored highlights and dark-framed glasses. She was pretty, and, as Polly had said, she seemed "posh," judging by the clothes and the accent. And the huge sailboat in the background. "We're excited to announce what's next for us."

"We're about to start off on an incredible adventure," Paul said. He wore jeans and a checkered button-down rolled up at the sleeves, and with his prep-school hair and classically handsome face, he had a casually messy appearance that said he didn't have to try all that hard.

"I've always loved sailing, and sailing around the UK is a dream I've had for many years," Annie said. "Just the two of us, and of course Mercedes. Say hi, Mercedes!" There was a shot of Annie cuddling the little Yorkie.

"Follow along with us on our adventures and misadventures as we take the journey of a lifetime." Paul grinned at the camera.

"Like I said, they gained a ton of followers since they started the boat thing," Polly said when the video ended. "But they had a pretty decent following before that too."

"What did you say they made videos about before the boat thing?"

"Oh, whatever. Their lives, their 'work.'" Polly made air quotes with her fingers. "Charity events. That kind of thing. If you scroll down, all the old videos are there. But be careful, you can lose hours this way."

"You've told Van you know who they are, right?" Harriet asked.

"Of course. He said they probably would have figured it out eventually, but I know he was pleased. I guess all my scrolling into rabbit holes finally paid off."

"I was just wondering if there was anything in their videos that would explain... I don't know. I don't suppose they made a video about abandoning ship, did they?"

"If they did, they haven't posted it yet," Polly said. "I've watched all their stuff, and there's nothing like that. I really hope they're okay."

"I suppose that wouldn't make sense anyway," Harriet said. If they'd been swept overboard in that storm, they would hardly have been able to film it, let alone post it on their channel.

"But you should watch their videos anyway," Polly said. "They're entertaining enough. Go on, start with the one at the top, where they show off the boat."

Harriet had to admit she was curious about the journey that had led them to this part of the coast. She pushed play.

"This is our boat, the *Salacia*," Annie said to the camera. "It belonged to my grandfather. He spent so much time down here at the marina when I was a kid. We took some short trips on it when I was young, but I've always wanted to take a longer journey, and this is finally our chance. We've been working on getting the boat fixed up and in tip-top shape." In the background of the video, Paul sat in the driver's seat, looking down at a computer screen that was built into the steering console. "Come on, I'll show you."

The camera followed her as she stepped onto the deck of the boat. "She's about fifteen meters, which is a pretty big boat, but Pop Pop always liked to host big parties, so he needed the space. We've redone the inside since his day, of course. Come see." She walked down the steps into the cabin, and the camera panned around the space Harriet had seen yesterday, only it was pristine in the video. The drawers and cabinets were all closed, and there were no glasses or dishes or clothing anywhere.

"This is our living room slash dining room slash kitchen," Annie said to the camera. "The upholstery was all beat up and from another century, so we had it redone in white leather, and I just love it." She gestured at the benches around the table and the couch area. Mercedes was sleeping on one of the couches. "The kitchen is small, but it's functional. There's a minifridge here, and a stove, and even a dishwasher." She showed off the features of their kitchen and then moved on to the bedrooms, but Harriet's mind was stuck on something Annie had said. The upholstery wasn't white leather—at least it hadn't been when Harriet was on board the boat yesterday. It was canvas of some kind. Wasn't it?

"Here are the bedrooms," Annie said. "As you can see, barely big enough for a double bed, but I always sleep so well on boats. And this one"—she gestured at the other bedroom—"is the spare, so come visit us!"

She spent the rest of the video talking about the boat and their trip and how they planned to set off from Plymouth, on the southern edge of England, where her grandfather had kept the boat. They would make stops on the coast as they worked their way counterclockwise around the UK. "Well, just England, Wales, and

Scotland—sorry Northern Ireland, you're too far!" Annie laughed and then carried the camera back above deck, where Paul was untying a rope that held one of the sails in place. "Make sure to tune in and follow along as we embark on this great adventure!"

"Is their dog okay?" Polly asked. "Is Mercedes lost at sea too?"

"Oh, Mercedes is fine," Harriet said. "She was alone on the boat when we found it. I've got her at my place until we locate her owners."

"Mercedes is *here*?" Polly's voice rose an octave.

"Yeah. I didn't bring her over because she's been through a lot, but she's just on the other side of the wall, sleeping peacefully."

"Oh my goodness. Can I meet her?"

"Uh, yeah?" Why was Polly so excited about meeting this dog?

"I'm sorry, it's just that, like, she's totally famous. I've never met a famous dog before."

Harriet went back to her place, found the little dog, and returned to the clinic.

"Oh my goodness, she's even cuter in real life!" Polly shrieked. Mercedes quivered but relaxed when Polly started scratching her head. "I can't believe how casual you are about this. This dog is so famous, and you didn't even think to mention it."

"I didn't know she was famous," Harriet said.

"Oh yeah, she shows up in so many of their videos. Here, I'll show you. They get more interesting when they're actually on their trip." Polly pointed at the screen. "Scroll down. Okay, here, click on this one."

Harriet clicked on the video and watched as Annie and Paul tied up their sailboat and announced, "We're at our first stop, in the village of Falmouth, here on the coast of Cornwall." They talked about the journey from Plymouth to Falmouth as smooth sailing, with strong winds pushing them in the right direction.

"How far apart are Plymouth and Falmouth?" Harriet asked. Her grasp of British geography was still pretty shaky.

"Not far. A couple of hours by car, maybe?" Polly answered. "But I have no idea what that would be in a boat."

Annie and Paul then showed footage from the village of Falmouth, which appeared to be an adorable fishing village with narrow streets filled with quaint shops and cafés. Annie went shopping, while Paul visited the local pub, and they talked with several people about how they were sailing around the UK. It seemed to come up even when it didn't necessarily need to, which Harriet found interesting. The video ended with them back on the boat and settling in for the night with a home-cooked meal and a view of the sunset.

"Doesn't seem too bad now, does it?" Polly said. "I wouldn't mind taking time off to sail around the country."

"It does look pretty wonderful," Harriet agreed. Most people—Harriet included—would never be able to take several months off work and sail around the country, or anywhere close to that, but it was kind of fun to see what it would be like. Sitting shotgun in Kyle's boat was as close as Harriet would likely ever come. "Must be nice to have a trust fund."

"No kidding."

"Is there a third person on the boat with them?"

"I don't think so. Why?"

"Some of the shots show both of them."

"Selfie stick," Polly said. "Or tripod, depending."

"With a phone. That makes sense." She should have figured that out.

"Yeah. That's how they do it."

Polly pointed to the next video, and Harriet clicked on it. It was a video of Annie and Paul at sea. Paul explained what the different ropes did and how he positioned the sails to try to catch the wind. There were plenty of shots of Annie standing on the bow of the boat with the wind blowing through her hair as golden sunlight dappled the water all around them. The next video was about them visiting a town called Newlyn, which was another old-fashioned fishing village with a large harbor. After that was a video showing them tying up at one of the Isles of Scilly—a place Harriet had never heard of, but Annie explained that it was an archipelago off the coast of Cornwall. They tied up in St. Mary, the largest and most populous of the islands, and the video showed scenes of them exploring the main city of Hugh Town, as well as lounging on the sandy beaches.

"It almost looks like the Caribbean," Harriet said, looking at the turquoise water.

"Not quite as warm though," Polly said.

"You get quite a nice look at the different places they go, don't you?" Harriet said when the video ended. She had learned a lot about two places she'd known nothing about. "It's like a tour book and geography lesson all in one. I can see why people like these videos."

"These early ones are nice, but they get more interesting as they go along. You should keep watching."

As Polly spoke, the bell over the front door dinged, and she jumped up.

"That'll be Mrs. Birtwhistle with Mittens. He needs a refill on his prescription, so I booked him for a checkup."

"Thank you, Polly." Harriet sighed. Somehow, she'd managed to waste most of her lunch hour, and she'd only seen a few videos. She'd watch more later, especially if—as Polly said—they got more interesting as they went along. For now, though, Mittens was waiting.

Harriet managed to keep focused for the most part on the pets she was tasked with caring for that afternoon, but when it was finally time to close up, she couldn't deny she was a tiny bit glad. She had plenty of paperwork to do, and she should get started on dinner, but she might watch a video or two before she really got going. She and Polly finished cleaning the exam rooms and waiting area and fed the two cats who were boarding at the clinic. As she was about to lock up, Van walked in to pick up Polly.

"Hi." Polly grabbed her purse and slung it over her shoulder. "Ready?"

"Hi, Van." Harriet waved, but she had a thought. If Van was here, she wasn't about to let him get away without a few questions. "Hey, is there any update on the missing sailors?"

She expected him to tell her that he couldn't say anything about an open investigation or something along those lines, but what he said was, "Actually, there's good news."

CHAPTER FIVE

"What's the good news? Did you find them?" Harriet asked.

"No, unfortunately, that's not it," Van said. "But we did determine that there are supposed to be eight life jackets on board that sailboat and there are only six. Plus, we found paperwork that says there should be an inflatable life raft on board—you know, the portable, inflatable kind—but there isn't. So hopefully, wherever they are, they have life jackets on and are in a life raft."

"But they still need to be found," Harriet said. "Are they any closer to being located?"

"Not so far." Van scrubbed a hand across his chin. "You have to understand, it's a needle in a haystack situation. Rescuers are searching everywhere. But given how vast the search area is—and it gets bigger by the hour as the currents push them farther and farther into the North Sea—it's going to be incredibly hard to locate them."

"I'm with Harriet," Polly said. "What's the good news?"

"The good news is that there's a chance," Van said.

When they both looked at him dubiously, he added, "Also, we're working on getting into the laptop that was left behind. We're hoping there may be some clue on it that will help."

"How would their laptop be able to tell you where in the ocean they're currently floating?" Polly asked.

"We don't know what we'll find," Van said. "Maybe nothing. But we've gotten permission from a judge to try to get in, in case there's something useful. Our forensic tech team is working on it now."

Harriet wondered, like Polly, how much it could possibly help if Paul and Annie were clinging to a life raft floating in the ocean, but she didn't say that. What Van had just said gave her an idea.

"What about their cell phones?" They obviously had them on board the boat. Where were they now?

"We haven't found any," Van said. "And we've searched every inch of that boat, so I don't think they're on board."

"That's odd, isn't it?"

"I don't think so," Van said. "If you're thinking they were suddenly swept overboard in a storm, maybe it's strange, but then again, everyone seems to have their phones with them all the time, right? If they had time to put on life jackets and inflate a life raft, they probably had time to grab their phones."

"And they would have taken them, to try to call for help," Polly said.

"But there haven't been any calls from them, right?" Harriet asked.

"None that we know of," Van said. "Nothing to 999." That was the British equivalent of 911. "But they may be out of range, depending on how far out they are. Coverage gets spotty once you get more than twenty or thirty kilometers from the coast."

"Are you able to track their phones? To see where they are?" Harriet used a tracking app to know where her devices were, and it also showed her where Will was—or at least where his phone was, which was almost always with him.

"We're trying to get in touch with family and friends, and if one of them has been tracking Paul's or Annie's phone, we might have some luck. We need a judge to approve getting access to their mobile records, which will tell us if their phones have pinged any nearby towers or whether they've made any calls or sent any texts. We're working on that now."

"How long will that take?"

"Hopefully not too long," Van said. "Depends."

Depends? "On what?"

Van shrugged. "How quickly we can get our request in front of a judge. The team is working on it."

Harriet didn't know if Van was being intentionally opaque or really didn't know, but either way, she wasn't going to get any more from him on this now. It was an active police investigation, after all, and there were limits to what he could tell her.

"Ready, Polly?" Van said.

"Ready." She popped up out of her chair. "Take good care of Mercedes."

"I will," Harriet said. "You guys have a good night."

She finished cleaning up and ushered Maxwell and Charlie through the door to the kitchen, where she found Will cooking what looked like some kind of pasta sauce. The smell of sautéed garlic and onions filled the room. He wore her frilly apron over his slacks and button-down, and a big smile.

"Hi, honey. How was your commute?"

Harriet smiled. He loved that joke.

"The commute was a bear. But I'm glad I made it." She walked over to the stove and kissed him. "It smells good in here."

"Thank you. I'm making my famous spaghetti and meatballs."

"If it's so famous, why haven't I heard about it?"

"Okay, it's soon to be famous. I've actually never made it before, but it's going to be good."

"That sounds lovely." She'd planned to make chicken for supper, but she couldn't complain about not having to cook. "How was your day? Did your meetings finish early?"

While Harriet tossed a salad, Will talked about a budget meeting and a lunch he'd had with a parishioner. Harriet bit her tongue as he tossed the pasta into a pot of water that wasn't quite boiling, and when he poured it into a colander a few minutes later, it didn't look done. Soon, they were seated at the table, and after Will blessed the food, he asked her about her day. She told him about treating Nellie the potbellied pig and about seeing the giant tortoise who was older than his owner. She tried her best not to show any sign that the pasta was crunchy and the meatballs were burned on the outside and nearly raw inside. She appreciated that Will wanted to make dinner, even if it didn't turn out perfectly.

"Wow. A tortoise? You don't see many of those around here," Will said. He cocked his head. "Actually, wait. I remember hearing about one. I don't remember the details, but it's something about a tortoise going missing in a shipwreck."

"Tortoises don't often sail."

"I don't think the tortoise was driving the boat," Will said. "Though if he had been, that might help explain why the boat sank."

"Are you sure this wasn't a dream?"

"I'm not sure. Maybe I'm making it up. Or maybe it was something that happened at Muckle Roe." He was referring to the

Scottish island his parents were from and where his father now lived. "But I don't think so. Maybe ask some of the old-timers around here about it."

"If you say so," she said dubiously.

Will laughed. "Or don't. I can hear how odd it sounds."

After they'd finished, Will stretched his arms up over his head. "It's such a beautiful night. Let's go for a walk."

"That sounds nice." A walk along the cliff trail would clear her head, as well as give her some good exercise. "Let's just get these dishes cleaned up first." They could load the plates and silverware into the dishwasher, but there were still all the pots and pans to take care of.

"We can do that afterward," Will said. "Let's go out before it gets dark."

Harriet hesitated. It would still be light for at least another hour, and she hated to leave dirty dishes in the sink to clean up later. She didn't want to do them now, but she wouldn't want to do them when they got back either, and she'd always thought getting unpleasant tasks out of the way first made everything else go more smoothly.

"Wouldn't you rather get it done?" She tried to keep the plaintive tone out of her voice. "I really have a thing about dirty dishes left in the sink."

Will hesitated. "Honestly, I'd rather enjoy the evening with my beautiful wife, but if it'll make you stressed to leave the dishes in the sink, let's do them now."

"Thank you." She got up from the table, grateful for her husband and his sensitivity. They were different people, with different ways of doing things. There was nothing wrong with that. It just meant they needed to continue to figure out how to live together.

Fifteen minutes later, they had the kitchen cleaned and wiped down, and they walked out of the house toward the path that ran along the cliffs. As they walked past Aunt Jinny's cottage, Harriet saw her in her garden, pruning the rosebushes.

"Lovely night for a walk, isn't it?" Aunt Jinny asked, smiling as they approached.

"It's beautiful," Harriet said. The air was warm, and the clouds were tinged pink and orange against the blue sky. "How are you?"

"Oh, I'm good. Busy day at the clinic, but I'm happy now." She snipped off a dead rose with her clippers.

"Anything interesting happen today?" Will asked. Harriet loved how he always took the time to ask people about what mattered to them.

"I suppose if you call a visit from the police interesting, sure."

"The police came to see you?" Harriet asked.

"What did you do this time?" Will put his hands on his hips and shook his head. Aunt Jinny laughed.

"It wasn't me this time," she said. "They came to ask me about diabetes. Did you hear about that couple that went missing from the sailboat out in the bay?"

"Yes, we were the ones who actually found the boat," Will said.

"Of course you did," Aunt Jinny said. "You always do manage to find your way into every perplexing mystery around here."

"This one was Will's doing," Harriet said. "But what does diabetes have to do with the missing sailors? Does one of them have diabetes?"

"The man, I guess. They believe type I—so the kind people can inherit or develop as a result of a virus or infection. They found an empty box for a bottle of insulin in the trash, but there wasn't one on the boat. There was also a sharps container half full of used syringes. They wanted to ask me how long he could go without it."

Oh. That was bad. That was very bad.

"You mean, the police wanted to know how long he could survive without it?" Harriet asked, her heart sinking.

"To be crass, yes," Aunt Jinny said. "If they're in a life raft somewhere, they could make it a few days without fresh water. Longer, if it rains. You can go more than a week without food. But if he's diabetic, and doesn't have insulin with him?" She shook her head. "It's not good."

"Wow." The urgency to find them had just grown exponentially.

"So that was my day," Aunt Jinny said. "I'm hoping one of you has something better to share about yours." She deadheaded another rose.

"I had a budget meeting," Will said, "so that wasn't great, but then I got to have lunch with Stephen Corbin, so that was nice."

Stephen Corbin. He was married to Ruby Corbin, who ran a fabric shop in town. They had two mischievous teenage sons.

"And how about you, Harriet?" Aunt Jinny asked. "Meet any interesting creatures today?"

"Actually, I did. There was a potbellied pig, and I also met a giant tortoise who is at least a hundred and twenty years old, but probably more. No one really knows."

"They live that long?" Will asked.

"The oldest living animal in the world—that we know of—is a giant tortoise," Harriet told him. "His name is Jonathan, and he's a hundred and ninety-two years young."

"That's amazing," Aunt Jinny said. "Still, a tortoise is an odd sort of pet for these parts. Where does this tortoise live?"

"The Baker farm," Harriet said. "It's mostly an alpaca farm, but apparently Jim has lived there since at least Rupert's great-grandfather's day. No one is quite sure how old he is or when he got there."

"The tortoise is named Jim?" Will laughed.

"Yes. That's what's carved into his shell, so that's apparently what he's called."

"I suppose it's as good a name as any for a tortoise," Will said. "Though I wonder why they carved the name into his shell. Doesn't that hurt him?"

"It would have at the time," Harriet said. "The good thing is, it doesn't hurt him now. And Rupert didn't know who carved the name, so the reason for it seems to have been lost."

Harriet's aunt wrinkled her brow, and she stared off at something in the distance.

"What is it, Aunt Jinny?"

"It's possible..." Her voice trailed off, and she scrunched up her nose.

"What's possible?" Harriet asked.

"Have you ever heard about the *Visiter*?"

"The what?"

"That's that shipwreck, right?" Will asked. "That's the one I was trying to remember!"

"That's right," Aunt Jinny said. She turned to Harriet. "The *Visiter*. It's a ship that went down off the coast in a big storm many years ago, just south of White Church Bay. Around 1880, I think. It's famous in these parts because of the dramatic and heroic effort of the villagers to rescue the sailors. They tried to launch a lifeboat from Whitby, but the waves were so bad they couldn't get out there. Instead, they decided to haul the lifeboat over land, through ice and snow, to bring it to White Church Bay to launch from here."

"They brought a lifeboat over the roads from Whitby in the snow?" Those roads were challenging enough normally, hilly and narrow, but at least they were paved these days, and generally not covered in snow and ice.

"I heard it took something like two hundred people and some ridiculous number of horses to get it here, but they made it," Will said.

"Indeed they did," Aunt Jinny said. "They launched the lifeboat from the spillway, and the volunteers from the Royal Naval Lifeboat Institution got there in time, and all the sailors were saved."

"That's incredible," Harriet said. There'd been plenty of shipwrecks in the area over the years, but she hadn't heard about this one.

"There's a plaque commemorating it, right on Station Road," Aunt Jinny said.

Harriet thought for a moment. "Is it that white sign by the benches?"

"That's the one," Aunt Jinny said.

"I've seen it but never stopped to read it," Harriet said.

"It's really pretty crazy, when you think about it," Will said. "It's incredible that they made it. And, if I remember correctly, it was the White Church Bay vicar who managed to get the message to the crew in Whitby that got the rescue underway." Will raised his chin and smiled, clearly pleased with his predecessor's role in the story.

"I'm glad to hear they made it," Harriet said. "But wait, what does any of this have to do with Jim the tortoise?"

"Oh, there's a rumor a tortoise went missing from the ship," Aunt Jinny said, shrugging, as if what she'd said wasn't at all strange. "They never saw it again."

"First off, why was there a tortoise on the ship?" Harriet asked.

"I don't know," Aunt Jinny said. "I suppose it was someone's pet or something."

"Who brings a pet tortoise on a ship?" Will asked.

"Or maybe it was some kind of cargo," Aunt Jinny continued. "You know how back in the day these old manor house guys were into exploring the world and were always bringing part of it home. All that Indiana Jones, *Heart of Darkness,* Elgin Marbles kind of stuff."

"You mean maybe it was part of the exotic animal trade," Harriet said.

"I guess so," Aunt Jinny said. "Or, I don't know. Maybe it was never there at all. Maybe it's all just a rumor. You're right, who would bring a turtle on a ship?"

"A tortoise."

"Aren't they the same thing?" Will asked.

"They're different species entirely," Harriet said. "Which is unfortunate, because turtles are amphibious, so they can swim, but tortoises are land animals. They don't swim."

"Well, I guess that's why they all thought it drowned," Aunt Jinny said. "But when you mentioned it, I wondered."

"Whether it's the same tortoise?" Harriet asked.

"It would be…what?" Will said. "A hundred and forty-five years old?"

"Something like that," Aunt Jinny said. "But you just said that Jim is at least a hundred and twenty years old. If they really do live that long, maybe it's possible? How many giant tortoises could there be around here?"

"Wouldn't that be wild?" Harriet said, laughing. "I wonder how we could figure out if it's the same animal." She thought about the lumbering tortoise she'd seen today. Was it possible? Could it have survived the shipwreck and lived all this time a few miles from the place where the ship went down? It was an intriguing question. "I'll see what I can find out."

"Well, let me know what you learn," Aunt Jinny said. "I'm curious now."

"I will," Harriet said. As they walked away, her mind swirled with questions. Will took her hand, and they wandered in silence to the path that led along the cliffs. The sun was starting to set, and the sky was lit up a brilliant pinkish-orange. Far below them, waves crashed against the base of the cliffs and the water dappled with the fiery orange glow of the reflected sky. For a moment, Harriet couldn't believe this was really her life. She couldn't believe she got to live here, in this magical place, with this amazing man.

"We're pretty lucky, aren't we?" Will asked.

"We are indeed," Harriet said. She leaned forward and kissed him.

They walked, hand in hand, up the path, and then, when the light started to fade from the sky, they turned around and headed back home.

When they got there, Will went into the living room to watch a soccer—football—game he'd recorded and Harriet sat down and opened her laptop. She wanted to do some research into the story of the shipwreck of the *Visiter* and see if she could learn anything about the tortoise that might have been on board. She spent a few minutes reading an account of the shipwreck and rescue.

She discovered that the *Visiter* was a brigantine. A web search for that word told her a brigantine is a kind of two-masted sailing ship. The pictures she saw online reminded her of the boat Christopher Columbus sailed, or like the one on *Pirates of the Caribbean*. Big, with a couple of masts and square sails, and possibly some jolly pirates swinging from the ropes. So, this brigantine was sailing from Newcastle to London in January 1881.

The *Visiter* was old, though, and apparently a strong storm tore the sails to shreds. The captain dropped anchor, hoping to ride out the storm, but the boat was pummeled by hail and snow, and the ship took on so much water that it began to break up and the crew of six men had to evacuate. They sheltered in the ship's rowboat and clung to a buoy, spending the night trying to stay upright in the terrible storm.

It wasn't until parts of the ship washed up on the beach at White Church Bay the next morning that anyone realized there'd been a shipwreck and that the six men clinging to their little boat could be seen far in the distance from the water's edge. The White Church Bay lifeboat was determined to be unfit to battle the waves, so the vicar sent a message to Whitby, pleading for them to send help from the larger port up the coast. The conditions made it too treacherous to make the journey by sea, so the decision was made to portage the boat six miles over land that rose to five hundred feet and then dropped back to sea level. It took eighteen horses and two hundred volunteers three hours to go those six miles to White Church Bay, struggling through snowdrifts up to eight feet deep. They launched the lifeboat successfully, but the terrible waves snapped six of the oars, and they had to return to shore. It was sent out once more, with fresh volunteers and new oars, to row the arduous journey, and was ultimately successful in rescuing all six men. They were brought safely to shore and treated for exposure, but they all survived the ordeal. After this, White Church Bay was outfitted with a newer, safer lifeboat that the RNLI used to rescue sailors in danger until 1931.

It was a very dramatic story, and she was glad to know that all six sailors survived the shipwreck. But there was no mention, in this account, of a tortoise. She kept poking around online, but there wasn't really very much about this old shipwreck on the internet. She supposed that if she wanted to learn more about the fate of the tortoise, she would need to look elsewhere. She decided she would make a trip to the library in the morning.

She pulled up Annie and Paul's social media channel and started watching some of their videos again. A short ad played before each video, but Harriet tuned them out. The next video after their stop in the Isles of Scilly was in a town called Padstow, which was another quaint fishing village on the coast of Cornwall. There was a shot of Mercedes, tucked under Annie's arm as they strolled through the streets. Harriet started to wonder how long before the videos would start feeling repetitive, though so far they'd managed to make each little town look unique and interesting.

The next video was different though. The title was DISASTER! Well, that was intriguing. What kind of disaster had they faced? Harriet clicked on the arrow and saw that it was another at-sea video, but in this one, Annie was alone in the small kitchen, looking around at open drawers and cabinets and a spilled milk container on the floor. Mercedes lapped at the puddle of milk.

"As you can see, we've got a bit of a mess here," Annie said. "It seems Paul forgot to latch the cabinets after breakfast this morning, and now you can see why it's important to do so. We hit some chop leaving the harbor this morning, and all the doors and drawers just flung open. We won't have milk until we get to a shop in Milford Haven. I'll post more about that journey in a separate video—if I don't kill my husband first, that is."

Calling it a disaster was a bit overblown. Some spilled milk was hardly a catastrophe, and the drawers and cabinets could be closed. She imagined Paul probably learned his lesson. But the video, she noticed, had the most views of any of their entries so far. That, despite the fact that it was far less interesting than the tours of the coastal cities, at least to Harriet's mind. There were more comments underneath as well—some people complained that, as Harriet thought, the title was misleading, while others sympathized with Annie about their husbands' foibles or offered "helpful" suggestions on how to remember to keep the doors latched next time. Harriet scanned the comments, decided there was nothing interesting there, and moved on to the next video.

This one, as Annie had promised, was about their trip from Padstow to Milford Haven. The video opened in pitch-black darkness, and Annie told the camera that they had just cleared the Padstow marina and were leaving at four a.m. to catch the tides both there and at their next stop. "As you can see, it's still dark out," she said to the camera. "This is our first time sailing in total darkness, and it's also our longest stretch at sea to date. We'll have to go about seventy nautical miles today, and most of that is out of sight of the coast, across the opening of the Bristol Channel, so we're sending up a lot of prayers that all goes well. I have to admit, I'm worried that until it gets light out, we're going to miss seeing something that's not lit up or get caught up in pot marker lines, but so far so good."

Harriet knew that what Annie was referring to in that last bit was that she was worried about getting their boat's motor caught in the ropes that connected lobster traps to the buoys that floated at the surface, since they wouldn't be able to see the buoys in the dark.

The next shot cut to Paul sitting at the steering console, looking at a couple of screens that glowed brightly against the steely sky. Morning was on its way in this shot, but it was still mostly dark out.

"Do you want to tell them what these are?" Annie asked Paul.

"This one is our navigation software," Paul said, pointing to a screen that showed a map of the area. "It tells us if we're on course. This other one"—he pointed to a second screen—"tells us about our location—GPS coordinates, that kind of thing."

"Can you tell us how you're feeling about the journey so far?" Annie asked.

"I'll feel a lot better once we get past Bristol Harbor," Paul said. "It's supposed to be pretty rough going once you're fighting those currents. The motor will be gunning, for sure."

There were a few more shots as the sky brightened, one of Annie laughing as dolphins swam alongside the boat, and one of Mercedes in a tiny dog-sized life vest. Then, some shots of the boat pitching and rolling, as promised, as they passed the entrance to Bristol Harbor. Harriet wondered why they didn't stop in the harbor, as they seemed to stop in most every marina they passed, but that wasn't explained. Maybe it was only for larger ships. Then there were more shots of the open sea and a look at the captain's logbook that Harriet had spotted on the boat. Paul had recorded what happened at various points in the journey:

4:00 Cleared Padstow harbor
4:30: Heard over the radio that the Coastguard is sending a lifeboat to someone. Didn't catch why.
5:17: Saw lights of another boat to starboard, stayed clear
5:30: Sky starting to brighten, don't think we caught any lines in the dark, thank goodness
6:20: Wind is strong NW, unfurled jib
7:47: Strong spray

Mixed in with the words were several long chains of numbers, which Harriet thought recorded their position. The video only showed the first page of the notes about their journey, but Harriet assumed there were more, because it was evening when they finally entered the marina at Milford Haven. Annie stood on the bow as Paul tied up the boat, and they signed off, promising to make another video to share more about the town once they'd had a chance to rest and explore.

"Are these the missing sailors?" Will asked, coming up behind Harriet. She'd told him on their walk about Polly showing her their channel.

"It's weirdly fascinating," Harriet said. "It's also... I don't know. Haunting, somehow."

"What do you mean?" Will asked.

"They're real people. I mean, obviously I knew real people had been on board when we saw their boat yesterday, but seeing them like this now, it makes them feel more real. They have personalities and hopes and fears, just like anybody else. Seeing their videos, it makes me even more worried about them."

"You have such a tender heart," Will said. "I love that about you."

He held out his hand, and when she took it, he pulled her to her feet.

"They'll find them," Will said. "They're out there somewhere, and they will be found."

Harriet hoped he was right. But if they were out there on a life raft somewhere, clinging to hope, they were running out of time.

CHAPTER SIX

Tuesday morning Harriet started the day at a farm, tending to a horse with a cut on its leg, but as soon as she got to the clinic, she decided she had time to watch one video before her first patient arrived. She had retrieved her laptop and was sitting in the waiting room when Polly entered.

"Hey," Harriet said as Polly closed the door. "Any news from Van about the boaters?"

"Nothing," Polly said. She nodded at the screen. "Watching Annie and Paul?"

"I keep thinking watching them might give me some idea about what happened to them somehow, though I know that makes no sense." Harriet sighed. "Maybe because there's nothing else I can really do, and this feels like I'm doing something."

"It's okay to be a fan. They've got plenty of those."

"I don't know that I'd say I'm a fan—"

"'Course, they've got plenty of haters too, but you're not hate-watching the videos, right?"

"What? No, I'm not hate-watching the videos." She didn't have the time or mental energy for that. "Wait, I guess I didn't realize they had a lot of haters."

"Oh, yeah. Take a look at the comments."

Harriet scrolled down and saw that Polly was right. Mixed in with comments about how great the videos were and how much viewers enjoyed them were comments about how fake Annie and Paul were. Some of the comments were merely rude, but others were downright hateful.

"Why do people dislike them so much?" Harriet asked.

"Because it's the internet, and some people are horrible online," Polly said with a shrug. "But also, because they think that all of this is just a show of how much money they have and they should get real jobs and contribute something worthwhile to society."

"But then how could they watch videos about a couple sailing around the country on a small yacht?" Harriet laughed. "It's a tough job, but somebody's gotta do it."

"Yeah, I mean, you know what you're gonna see when you click on the video, right?" Polly nodded. "I think it's nice to see something new and interesting. I'll probably never be able to afford to do something like that, but it's nice to live vicariously through them as they do it."

The bell over the door dinged, and Polly shrugged and said, "Back at it." She greeted their first patient and escorted the man and his cat to an exam room, but there were a few more minutes before the appointment officially started, so Harriet scanned some additional comments.

Lying Fakes.
Why do you try so hard to be someone you're not?
Pathetic losers.

The comments were harsh, and Harriet was tempted to ignore them, but a part of her wondered... What did people think they were lying about?

There were also recent comments that showed that their fans had learned about their disappearance.

We're praying for you, Annie and Paul!
Did you guys hear that Annie and Paul are LOST @ SEA?
Vanished right off their boat. What?!
Stay strong. We're rooting for you.

She scrolled to the most recent video and looked the comments over, and it was more of the same. Lots of vitriol, not a lot of facts, plus some well-wishes from fans who had heard the news. But there was one comment that caught her attention.

That's not your grandfather's boat, Annie. Why do you lie about things that can be verified? It was posted by someone called AnthonyMag.

What did that mean? Why wouldn't it be her grandfather's boat? Why did AnthonyMag think it wasn't? Why would Paul and Annie lie about it?

Harriet had learned about boat registration numbers a few months before when she investigated that mystery involving smuggling. The numbers were used to track who owned what boat. The problem was that the information wasn't publicly available. Only the police or government authorities had access, in the same way that an everyday citizen couldn't look up car ownership by searching a license plate number. But if she could find the registration number of Paul and Annie's sailboat, maybe she could ask Van for more information.

She was pretty sure...yes, there in the first video, was a sideview of the front of the boat. And there, clearly visible, was a code made up of one letter and three numbers. H593.

H. Harriet tried to remember what Will had told her the letters in registration numbers stood for. She was pretty sure they corresponded with the port where the boat was registered. She didn't recognize *H*, but a quick online search revealed that it was the code for Hull. That was a town right there in Yorkshire, a couple hours south of White Church Bay. Officially called Kingston upon Hull, it was an old port city with some beautiful buildings and a long history in the wool trade.

But wait. Hadn't Annie said that the boat was her grandfather's and it had been kept in Plymouth? She was pretty sure... Harriet rewound the video and watched it from the beginning. "This is our boat, the *Salacia*," Annie said. "It belonged to my grandfather. He spent so much time down here at the marina when I was a kid." Harriet fast-forwarded the video to the end, where Annie mentioned that they would begin their journey in Plymouth, where her grandfather had kept the boat.

So what did it mean that the boat was registered in Hull, not Plymouth?

Harriet heard Polly still going through their routine new-patient interview, so she decided she had time for a quick call. Will had grown up around boats. He knew this stuff.

He picked up on the first ring. "Hey, sweetheart."

"Is the port where a boat is docked also the port where it's registered? Or could there be a scenario where it lives in a different place than where it's registered?"

"Good morning to you too, my darling wife. How are you this fine morning?"

"Good morning, Will." Harriet sighed. She supposed it hadn't been the best way to greet her brand-new husband.

"You know, I can hear you through the wall," Will said. "Why didn't you just come back here to ask?"

"I've got a patient waiting. I just have a few seconds, and I really need to know."

"Ah. An emergency boat registration question. You'd be surprised how often those come up."

"Will."

"Okay, okay. Yes, the port where a boat is registered should be where it's regularly docked. I can't say it would never happen any other way, but it would be unusual."

"That's what I thought."

"I'm assuming this has something to do with the missing sailors?"

Polly poked her head in the doorway and mouthed, "They're waiting," with a toss of her head toward the exam room.

"Yep. Thanks! Gotta run, but I'll see you later!" Harriet hung up, slipped her phone into her pocket, and rushed to the first exam room, where Noodle, a tan and white cat, waited with his owner. Noodle was there for a routine checkup.

The morning was busy, but when they had a short break between patients, Harriet told Polly what she'd discovered.

"So there really is a reason people think they're fakes?" Polly asked.

"I don't know," Harriet said. "Just that something she said in a video doesn't seem to match up with reality. It's possible I'm misunderstanding or that there's a simple explanation for it."

"You should call Van," Polly said. "Maybe they already know that her grandfather kept the boat at the Plymouth marina, but just in case..."

Harriet was thinking the same thing. "I'll call him now."

She called Van's cell phone, but when he didn't pick up, she left a voice mail telling him what she'd learned about Annie saying the boat was docked at Plymouth, not Hull. Then she went into the exam room to see Scarlett, an Irish setter she'd seen a few months back for a skin condition. After Scarlett, it was time to take a break for lunch.

"I'm going to run to the library," Harriet told Polly.

"Have fun!" Polly waved at her and kept typing.

The library was in the upper part of town, housed in a stone cottage with big white shutters. Harriet parked, walked inside, and then looked around, trying to figure out where to start.

"Hello, Harriet." Oliver, one of the librarians, greeted her. He was younger than she was, with curly hair and wire-rim glasses. "Looking for anything in particular?"

"I'm looking for information about an old shipwreck," Harriet said. "The *Visiter*. In particular, I'm interested in learning about a tortoise that I've heard was on board when the ship sank."

"A tortoise?" Oliver said. "That's a new one."

"You never heard about a tortoise who drowned in the shipwreck?"

"It wasn't ever mentioned in the stories I've heard," Oliver said. "But I certainly don't know everything about it."

"It may not be true. Aunt Jinny said she'd heard about it, so I'm trying to find out if there's any possibility there really was a tortoise on board. Do you have any idea where I should look?"

"Let's see." He pursed his lips then said, "I'd start with the local history section. There are a couple of books there that mention the *Visiter*, I think." He tapped his fingers on the counter. "And I suppose you could look at the contemporary newspaper accounts, to see if the tortoise is mentioned in those."

"Those would be in the newspaper archive?" Harriet asked.

"That's right," Oliver said. "I can show you where that is, if you like."

"I'll see if I can figure it out," Harriet said. "I'll let you know if I have any trouble. But I'll start with the local history."

"Good luck."

Harriet made her way to the small endcap display of books about Yorkshire. She found one entitled *Shipwrecks of the Yorkshire Coast*. She took that one, as well as a book about important sites in Yorkshire put out by the North Yorkshire Moors Association, and sat down at a nearby table to look through them.

She flipped open the first one and began skimming the pages. She knew the quickest way to the information she sought was to consult the index, but it was fascinating, and also sobering, to see that there had been so many shipwrecks over the years. She supposed the whole region used to rely on fishing and shipping, and with the craggy coastline and unpredictable weather, shipwrecks must have been somewhat inevitable. But it was still startling to read about them, one after another.

There was the *Bonhomme Richard*, whose captain, John Paul Jones, famously declared, "I have not yet begun to fight" before defeating the British *Serapis*, transferring his crew to it, and allowing his own badly damaged ship to sink. There was the *Wolfhound*, which went down near the coast of Whitby in 1896. The SS *Rosa*, which ran aground in 1930. There was the 1885 wreck of the Russian cargo ship *Dmitry* that inspired Bram Stoker to create one of the most famous shipwreck survivors of all time in his character Dracula. That book was mostly set in Whitby. There was the 1861 incident in which twelve men drowned when their lifeboat flipped over after rescuing sailors from a sinking ship. The only survivor of that accident was wearing a new-fangled invention called a life jacket. There was the fishing trawler the *Sarb-J*, which ran aground in 1994. Up until fairly recently, most of the ship was visible at low tide, and she remembered seeing it on visits to her grandfather when she was a kid, though the ship had broken up in recent years.

There was also an entry for the *Visiter*, and Harriet slowed down and read through it carefully. It gave her more context than what she'd read online. She learned, for instance, that the ship was carrying a load of coal when it went down, and that it was locally owned and registered to a captain named Trueman Robinson. She learned that, after the rescue, the RNLI gave the lifesaving station that now stood by the spillway a new, seaworthy lifeboat called *Ephraim and Hannah Fox*. But there was nothing about a tortoise.

She set that book aside and paged through the second book. She smiled when she found an entry describing the delightfully strange coin-collecting cod in town. The statue of the cod stood on its tail with its mouth open wide. A sign above it asked for donations to the Royal National Lifeboat Institution. Harriet had seen the statue in town, and even put a few coins in the fish's mouth, because how could she not? Now she read that the statue had been there since 1887.

The book also highlighted the sites of the collection points in Yorkshire for the Shipwrecked Mariner's Society, an organization that provided financial assistance to "fishermen and mariners and their dependents who have suffered hardship, misfortune or poverty, as a result of an accident, illness, disability, unemployment or retirement." She read that the organization was started in 1839, and that sixty collection boxes were scattered around the UK's coastline. The "boxes" were actually old sea mines that had been painted red and white.

There was also an entry in the book for the *Visiter* plaque on Station Road. But that was it. Nothing new about the shipwreck itself, and certainly nothing about a tortoise.

"No luck?" Oliver asked when he saw her returning the books to the shelves.

"I'm afraid not," Harriet said. "I'll try the newspapers."

"I'll get you set up." Oliver helped her pull up the searchable newspaper archive and set the parameters for her search. "You're looking for newspapers that would have been published at the time of the wreck?" he asked.

"Yes, please." Harriet watched as he set the date to January 1881 and chose to search all newspapers in Yorkshire. She then typed in the word *Visiter* and hit return. Links to several articles came up, and Harriet clicked on the first one. It was an article published on Wednesday, January 19, in *The Whitby Gazette*.

Brigantine Visiter Sinks off Coast of White Church Bay, All Sailors Safe

The article itself recalled the daring rescue but didn't include any information she hadn't already found. The follow-up issue, which was published January 26, contained several headlines about the shipwreck. Lifeboat Volunteers Commended for Bravery, announced one, and Pieces of Wrecked Ship Wash Ashore After Doomed Journey, said another. The second article reported that part of the ship's hull and a portion of its mast had been brought to shore by the waves following the storm. That was interesting, but the article didn't contain anything relevant to her search.

When she scrolled down, she found links to a story in *The Scarborough Mercury*, a newspaper that wasn't around anymore. She clicked on the link, which brought her to a digitized version of the front page from January 22, 1881. It was hard to read. There were dozens of headlines squashed onto the front page, each no more than a line or two under them, with stories continuing on later pages. She searched the headlines and found one that said Captain Tries to Reclaim Cargo from Visiter Washed Up on Beach.

Harriet squinted so she could read the article.

> *Objects recovered from beaches stretching from Ravenscar to Whitby have all been claimed by Trueman Robinson, captain of the ship* Visiter *that sank off the coast of White Church Bay last week. Several unopened barrels of liquor and flour were found just below White Church Bay, and many wooden boxes containing coal have also been recovered, as well as several of the sailors' personal items, including a silver comb*

said to belong to the first mate. The items have been claimed by Robinson, who says they are his property as owner of the ship. He also tells this paper that many valuable items that were on board the ship are still missing, including a Japanese painted screen, a sapphire necklace, and a tortoise from the Seychelles Islands. The tortoise, a land animal, is believed to have drowned. Anyone encountering such items is asked to return them to Captain Robinson.

There it was. A mention of the tortoise after all. So, there *had* been one on board. Could Jim really be that missing tortoise?

But there was another question in her mind. Was Captain Robinson right in claiming that everything that washed up from the sunken boat was his? Had he recovered anything more? What about the sapphire necklace and the Japanese screen? And what were items like that doing on a ship that was supposed to be carrying coal? White Church Bay was rumored to have been a hub for smugglers back in the day. Was that why he had exotic items on board the ship? What was he really doing out there in the North Sea?

That was the end of the search results. She tried searching again, this time looking for "tortoise" and "shipwreck tortoise," but nothing else came up.

She stretched her arms up over her head. It was time for her to get back. She hadn't learned whether Rupert's tortoise was the *Visiter*'s tortoise, but at least she'd discovered that the rumors about a tortoise on board the ship were more than just rumors.

"Find what you need?" Oliver asked as she walked to the front of the library.

"I got a good start, anyway," Harriet said. "Though now I want to learn more about the captain of the boat and what he was up to. Do you happen to know anything about a Captain Trueman Robinson?"

"I don't think so," Oliver said. "But I can look around and see if I can find anything."

"That would be great," Harriet said. "Thank you."

She headed out of the library. Before she got to her car, she pulled out her phone and searched her contacts for Rupert Baker. Jim the tortoise's guardian. She called him and got in her car as it rang.

"Hello? Dr. Bailey?"

"Hi, Rupert. I'm sorry to bother you. I wanted to check and see how the llamas are doing."

"Yeah, they're good," Rupert said. "They don't really say much, but they seem to be doing just fine, from what I can tell."

"That's good. And how about Jim?"

"I don't mean to be cheeky, Doc, but if I have a hard time reading the emotional state of llamas, I don't know how you think I'd be able to tell anything about a tortoise. Jim seems pretty much the same as always, from what I can tell."

"In that case, it sounds like he's doing just fine," Harriet said, and then tried to bring the conversation around to the real reason she'd called. "I have to admit, I've been thinking a lot about Jim. You don't see too many giant tortoises around these parts. But my aunt Jinny told me about a tortoise that went missing from a ship that sank off the coast of White Church Bay in 1881. Have you heard of the shipwreck of the *Visiter*?"

"I'm afraid I haven't."

"After the ship went down, the captain said there was a tortoise on board. It was thought to have drowned, but now I'm wondering…"

"When did you say this shipwreck happened?"

"1881."

"Blimey. If Jim was on that ship, that would mean he's…"

"Even older than we thought," Harriet said. "But tortoises can live at least that long, so it's not impossible, not by any means. So I was wondering, is there any chance Jim is the tortoise that was on that ship?"

"I have no idea," Rupert said. "I suppose you'd have to ask him."

Harriet laughed.

"I wouldn't have the first clue how to find out if that's where he came from," Rupert said.

"Did your grandfather ever say anything about how or where Jim was found?" Harriet asked. "Pass along any family stories?"

"Not that I know of," Rupert said. "I can ask my mum, but she's not comprehending much of anything these days."

"If there is any way to find out what you can about where Jim came from, it would be wonderful to know," Harriet said.

"But how would Jim have made it from a shipwreck to my farm?" Rupert asked. "He can't swim."

"That's a question I would very much like to know the answer to," Harriet said. "If you come up with anything, will you let me know?"

"Of course," Rupert said. She thanked him and hung up.

She'd struck out on that call, but there were plenty of other avenues to examine. At the moment, though, she had a job to do. She returned to the clinic, where she found a wiggly dachshund puppy in the exam room waiting for its shots. Nothing cured frustration like holding a puppy, and she spent longer than she should have petting and snuggling the little guy. After she finally handed him back to his owners, she went on to treat a few cats and a series of rodents before she walked out into the waiting room to find DI Kerry McCormick and Sergeant Adam Oduba waiting for her.

"Good afternoon," she said, nodding at the officers. She'd interacted with the detective inspector while working on previous mysteries. DI McCormick was based in the county's headquarters and was called in when a crime went beyond the scope of what Van would typically handle.

Instead of greeting her in return, the inspector said, "Harriet, we're going to need you to come down to the station."

CHAPTER SEVEN

Harriet didn't know why she was being summoned to the station, but she figured the fact that she was allowed to drive her own car instead of being taken in a police car was a good sign.

Rationally, she knew she wasn't in trouble. She'd done nothing wrong. But DI McCormick wouldn't tell her what was going on, saying she would explain at the station, so Harriet couldn't help but worry. She strapped herself into her car and turned on the engine, leaving Polly to close up the clinic, but before she got going, she called Will to let him know what was going on.

"I'm actually headed there too," Will said. "Van came down to the church and asked me to come to the station to, as he put it, 'talk for a bit.'"

"Well, in that case, I feel a little bit better," Harriet said. "If we're under arrest, at least we'll both end up in the slammer together."

"We're not under arrest," Will said, laughing. "I'm pretty sure they just want to talk to us about what happened with the sailboat."

"We've told them what we know."

"Apparently, they want us to tell them again. I'm sure it's fine, Harriet. I'll see you there shortly."

Harriet knew he was right, but she was still nervous as she parked at the station and walked inside. She was led into a conference room and found both Will and Kyle seated at a long table.

"Hi, Kyle," Harriet said. She leaned over and planted a kiss on Will's cheek.

"I'm glad to see it wasn't just me," Kyle said nervously. "I thought I was in trouble when that officer showed up."

Harriet sat down and smiled at him. "I feel the same way."

"You'd think they'd have just called us," Will said. "It would have been more efficient."

They chatted about work for a while, and then DI McCormick walked in, followed by Sergeant Oduba and Van.

"Thank you all for coming in," the inspector said, taking a seat across from Harriet and the two men. Sergeant Oduba and Van sat down on either side of her, facing the three of them. "We have some questions for you about what you saw on the abandoned sailboat on Sunday."

"Of course," Will said. Harriet nodded her agreement.

"Can you please tell us what happened and what you saw, starting from the beginning?"

Harriet, Will, and Kyle took turns retelling the story of how they'd come upon the boat, what made them think there was something odd about it, how they'd heard a dog barking from inside as they got closer. Then Will and Harriet told them what they'd seen when they boarded the boat.

"Did you touch anything?" Sergeant Oduba asked.

"Not that I can think of," Harriet said. "Aside from the handrail as I walked down the steps to the lower level. Well, and the dog, of course. Will had picked her up when he got on the boat. When I got on, he handed her to me. I held on to her, because she was scared."

"Is the dog still in your possession?" the inspector asked.

"She is," Harriet said. "We couldn't leave her there, and the Coastguard officers thought it made sense for me to care for her until the sailors were found. She was hungry and thirsty, but she's doing just fine now."

"We didn't disturb anything on the boat," Will confirmed.

"Wait, actually, I did flip through the pages of the logbook they had on the counter in the kitchen," Harriet said. "I'm sorry about that, but I used the sleeve of my sweatshirt to cover my hands. I didn't leave any fingerprints."

"It was on the counter when you found it?" DI McCormick asked.

"That's right," Harriet said.

"Not by the driving console on the upper level?" Sergeant Oduba asked.

"No," Harriet said. "Definitely on the counter."

The sergeant wrote something in his notebook. Actually, now that he'd mentioned it, why was it on the counter? Was that a normal place to keep something like that?

"Did you notice anything odd about the logbook?" DI McCormick asked.

"I read the last entry, where it said they were in a storm and struggling to keep the boat upright," Harriet said. "Annie wrote it, and she said Paul was on deck, fighting to keep the boat steady."

"Did that seem odd to you?" Sergeant Oduba asked, his dark eyes focused on her.

"No. Eli, from the Coastguard, mentioned there was a storm out at sea on Saturday night," Harriet said. "Why? Was there something odd about it?"

None of the officers said anything to that, but the inspector wrote something down on her notepad.

"You didn't touch or move anything else?" she asked.

Harriet and Will both shook their heads.

"Did you look inside the refrigerator?" Van asked.

"No," Harriet said.

"You didn't take anything from the fridge?"

"No," Harriet told him, more emphatically this time.

"We definitely didn't take anything from the refrigerator," Will added. "We didn't open it or touch it. We were looking for people, so we had no reason to look in the fridge."

"Why? Was something missing?" Harriet asked, even though she thought she knew the answer. He was checking on that bottle of insulin they hadn't been able to find.

Instead of answering, DI McCormick asked, "Did you see any mobile phones on the boat?"

"No," Harriet said. "I asked Van about those the other day. It seemed odd to me that there weren't any."

The inspector flicked her eyes at Van and then down at her paper, but she didn't say anything.

"Can you tell us again what you did, exactly, when you went on board the boat?" she asked after a moment.

Will repeated how he'd searched the boat, explaining in which order he'd visited the rooms, and how he'd then returned topside and asked Harriet to come on board to check it out.

"Why did you feel like you needed a second set of eyes?" Sergeant Oduba asked, leaning back in his chair.

"Harriet is very good at noticing details," Will said. "She sees things a lot of people miss. But also, she's a vet, and there was a dog, so…"

The sergeant turned to Harriet. "Did you see anything Will missed?"

"Nothing that I haven't already told you about," Harriet said.

DI McCormick twisted the cap of her pen on and off. "Is there anything else you can think of? Anything you saw, or impressions you had that might tell us anything about what happened to Annie and Paul Bellingham?"

"Wait," Harriet said. "There was one thing." All eyes turned on her. "They lied in one of their videos about the interior of the boat," she told them. "Annie said in the video they'd had it redone in white leather. But when I saw it, it was clear it was just regular fabric."

"Why would they do that?" Will asked. "Why would they lie about such a thing?"

Harriet looked at DI McCormick expectantly, but the inspector was giving nothing away. She looked up from her notebook and said, "Anything else?"

"Not that I can think of." Harriet tried to parse the three officers' words, looking for anything that would indicate what she was missing. She couldn't figure it out, so instead, she decided to remind them of the clue she'd given them earlier. "Did you have any luck finding out who the boat is registered to and why the location doesn't match what Annie and Paul said in their video?"

"We're still looking into the boat's registration," DI McCormick said, making a notation on her pad.

She was still not giving anything away. Harriet tried again.

"Were you able to get in contact with Annie or Paul's family, to see about tracking their phones?"

"Our team is on it," DI McCormick said.

Which was neither a yes or a no. Harriet realized she was not getting anything out of the inspector.

"Is there anything else you need to know?" Kyle asked.

"No, I think that's about it for now," Sergeant Oduba said. "Thank you all for coming in."

"We appreciate your help," Van said, as the other officers gathered their papers and walked out. The four of them were left sitting there, and Harriet tried to figure out what had just happened.

"They know something, don't they?" Will asked Van. "The police know something about where the sailors are."

"We don't know where they are," Van said.

"That's not really answering the question." Harriet leaned forward and placed her forearms on the table.

"How about I walk you to your cars?" Van said.

They all stood, and as Kyle and Harriet walked to the door, Will went behind and pushed all their chairs in neatly. He was such an insanely nice guy, it was almost unreal. They followed behind Van as he led them through the station and out to the parking lot. They all walked to Harriet's behemoth of a vehicle.

"Look, I can't really tell you anything, obviously," Van said. "But your tip about the angry comment on the message board helped us out, so here's what I can tell you. We don't know where the Bellinghams are, but there are a lot of things that don't add up."

"Like the fact that the life raft and two life jackets are missing but they left their dog?" Harriet said.

"For one," Van said.

"And their phones being missing?" Will said.

"With the location tracking turned off," Van said, nodding. "We haven't been able to get in touch with any family. We got permission from a judge to get access to their mobile records, and there hasn't been any activity at all since Saturday. No calls, no texts, and no location information transmitted. No pings on cell towers."

"So, they've not only turned their location tracking off, they've turned their phones off altogether," Kyle said.

"Which is kind of an odd thing to do if you're in dire need of help clinging to a life raft," Will added.

"They could be completely out of service range," Van conceded. "Or it's possible their phones are lying on the bottom of the ocean—intentionally or not. But we have reason to believe that their disappearance isn't on the up-and-up."

"How?" Will and Harriet asked at the same time.

"We were able to get location data from the boat itself, and let's just say it's suspicious," Van said.

"Suspicious how?" Harriet said.

Van pressed his lips together, but then he said, "All right, here's what I can say. The boat's AIS signal was turned off two days before you found it."

Kyle must have seen the puzzled look on Harriet's face, because he said, "AIS—which stands for 'automatic identification system'—is like GPS for boats. Not all recreational boats are required to have it, but many large boats for ocean-going voyages do. This one did, which means the authorities should be able to track its movements."

Harriet connected the dots in her mind. "Could the equipment or whatever it is have malfunctioned?"

"It could have," Kyle said, "but there's no way they could have gone that long without knowing it wasn't working."

"He's right," Van said. "And the first thing they should have done when they knew there was a problem was take the boat in and get it fixed."

"So does that mean they purposefully turned off their signal and rode into a storm?" Harriet was incredulous. "Why in the world would they do that?"

"And does that mean they didn't want to be found?" Will asked. The look on his face matched what Harriet was feeling.

"These are all questions we're looking into." Van turned away, saying, "I should go in."

"Thanks, Van," Harriet said, but he was already walking toward the station. She watched as he went inside.

"So you really can turn off your location signal if you want to?" Harriet asked.

"Sure," Kyle said. "It's not a good idea, but you can."

An idea was forming in Harriet's mind. "What if they wanted us to think they'd been swept overboard in a storm?" she said slowly. "They wanted it to look like they were lost at sea."

"Why would anyone do that?" Will said, his eyes narrowed. "And why turn off their location if they wanted the abandoned boat found?"

"I don't know," Harriet said. "Maybe they turned it off so we wouldn't know where they'd gone or what they'd done before they left the boat. Maybe they want to get away with something and create new identities for themselves." She listened to herself and knew how crazy her theory sounded. But crazier things had happened. "The more I hear, the more I believe they didn't get swept overboard in a storm or have to abandon ship for some terrible reason. But they sure want us to think they did."

CHAPTER EIGHT

Harriet talked with Will and Kyle about what they'd just learned as they ate fish and chips from Cliffside Chippy. From the picnic tables outside the small restaurant, they had a great view of the Bay. Waves pounded away at the cliffs below them, and steely gray clouds hung ominously overhead, but the evening was dry and not too chilly.

"Why would they want people to think they'd been washed overboard in a storm?" Kyle asked. "What possible reason could they have?"

"Maybe Harriet's right," Will said. "They wanted to disappear." He took a bite of his fried fish and wiped his hands on his napkin. "Make it look like they were lost for good. Maybe start over somewhere else."

Kyle drenched his french fries in vinegar, which was a British thing Harriet would never understand. "But if they wanted to disappear," he said, "why would they do it in such a public way? Why not just slip away somewhere quietly?"

"They're public people," Harriet said. "Surely their audience would notice if they simply stopped making videos. Maybe this way they had a story that no one would question. Everyone would think they were dead."

"Would they have left Mercedes behind though?" Will asked. "If they wanted us to think they'd been swept out to sea, wouldn't we have just thought that the dog was too?"

"Which is another reason I'm not sure I'm buying the whole thrown overboard thing," Harriet said. "For some reason, they decided they didn't want a dog in this new life of theirs."

"That may be true," Kyle said, "but I would hope that at the very least they were thinking someone would find her and give her a good home."

"Not if they turned off the AIS signal," Will reminded him. "The question is, did they want the boat found? They might have wanted to delay that happening so they could get as far away as possible."

"Maybe they had a plan, but something went wrong," Harriet said. "I don't like to think of anyone just abandoning a pet."

"Or they might not have been the ones that made it look like they'd been swept overboard," Will said. "It's the logbook entry that tells us they were struggling in the storm, right?"

"That's right," Harriet said. "How do we know it really was Annie who wrote it?" Will asked. "Couldn't somebody else have added that after making sure Annie and Paul were gone from the boat somehow?"

"You mean someone kidnapped them?" Harriet asked.

"Or took them off the boat for whatever reason," Will said. "Maybe not kidnapped but taken somehow. I mean, obviously, I hope not. I'm just trying to think of possibilities that would make sense."

Kyle nodded. "In some ways, the idea of Annie and Paul being forcibly removed from the boat"—Harriet appreciated how Kyle rephrased what she was thinking—"is a scenario that fits the facts.

It doesn't make sense that they'd just abandon their boat on the sea, if you ask me. Even if they wanted to escape, even if they had some reason to want to start a new life, why would they simply abandon their boat like that? That thing costs as much as a small house. Why leave it to be smashed against the rocks? No one in their right mind would leave that behind to start a new life, right?"

"You'd sell the boat for cash and use that to start your new life, most likely," Will said, nodding.

"So maybe they're not the ones who turned the signal off," Kyle said. "If the bad guys didn't want anyone following them or finding them, then that's the first thing they'd do. And they'd make sure Paul's and Annie's phones were off. They kidnapped Annie and Paul in Sunderland, doctored the logbook, and then set the boat free to sail on its own—with Mercedes on board."

"Okay." Harriet absorbed this. "You're saying that if they didn't get swept overboard—which, it seems, is not looking likely—then maybe someone forced them to abandon their boat against their will. But who?"

"Pirates, maybe," Kyle said.

Harriet wanted to laugh, but then she saw that Kyle wasn't joking.

"I don't mean, like, Captain Jack Sparrow or Blackbeard or something like that," Kyle said.

"Which is too bad, because I imagined Johnny Depp swinging onto the deck of the *Salacia* with a cutlass," Harriet said.

"Or some of those people who show up at the Whitby Pirate Festival," Will said.

Kyle threw a french fry at him. "I mean actual pirates, who still sail the seas to this day," he said. "They're still a thing."

"They very much are," Will agreed. "A chunk of what the Coastguard does is help prevent smuggling and protect ships at sea, sometimes from pirates."

Harriet had heard about that in recent years. Thieves boarded ships, held the crew hostage, and stole the cargo. She didn't know how prevalent it was, but she knew it was still very much a threat to ocean-going vessels.

"So now we're thinking they were kidnapped by pirates?" Will asked.

"Or by someone else," Kyle said. "They've clearly got plenty of money. Maybe someone took them, hoping to get a ransom payment out of it."

"Annie does come from money," Harriet said. "And she has a trust fund."

"Maybe they've made enemies," Kyle said. "Or it's just someone who wants a payday."

"Holding people for ransom doesn't sound like something that happens in this day and age," Will said, shaking his head. "Not here in our area anyway."

"Not to mention, if that's the case, where's the ransom note?" Harriet pointed out. "It doesn't do a lot of good to hold someone for ransom unless you let their people know you have them so you can collect your money."

"Still, it might be worth considering," Will said. "Not pirates, exactly, but the idea that they were kidnapped or taken from the boat against their will."

"Again, it makes more sense than them abandoning their own boat at sea," Kyle said.

As unlikely as it sounded, Harriet couldn't argue that it was a possibility. But who would want to kidnap them, and why?

"Of course it could always be extraterrestrials," Will said. "I hear alien abductions are on the rise."

Harriet turned to look at him and saw that he struggled to keep a straight face.

"Or maybe they sailed into a Yorkshire version of the Bermuda Triangle," Kyle volunteered.

They were just trying to make her laugh now, and as ridiculous as they were being, she couldn't deny that she appreciated them trying to lighten the mood. If what the police suggested was right, and Annie and Paul weren't simply lost at sea, that suggested something far more sinister was going on.

She prayed they would find out what and bring them home safely.

CHAPTER NINE

On Wednesday morning, the missing boaters were on the front page of the *Whitby Gazette*. Harriet read the article while she waited for Maxwell and Mercedes to do their business in the yard, and then she carried the paper inside and read it more thoroughly.

SAILBOAT RECOVERED IN BAY; POLICE AND COASTGUARD SEARCH FOR MISSING BOATERS

HM Coastguard responded to a call reporting an abandoned sailboat in the water just south of White Church Bay on Sunday. The drifting boat was found by three WCB residents who were out for a day of fishing.

The Coastguard and dozens of volunteers have been searching the waters around White Church Bay, looking for any sign of the missing sailors, identified as Annie and Paul Bellingham, from London, who are social-media influencers. The couple were sailing around the UK in their boat, the Salacia, posting videos about their journey along the way on their social-media channel. Since the news of their disappearance broke on Sunday night, their fans have been flooding the couple's channel with comments offering support and good wishes.

"I can't believe this has happened to them," said a user identified as KeeleyFootieFan, in the comments below the couple's most recent video. "We hope they're found soon, safe and sound!"

"If you have any information about the whereabouts of Annie and Paul Bellingham, please alert the authorities immediately," said Detective Inspector Kerry McCormick.

That didn't really tell Harriet anything she didn't already know, unfortunately, except that they were still missing.

She didn't have any early-morning appointments, and Will left just after sunrise to visit a parishioner in the hospital, so after she ate breakfast and spent some time reading her devotions, she poured herself another cup of coffee and opened her laptop. She checked Annie and Paul's page, just to see if there were any updates, but all she found were more comments on the latest video.

Praying for you from Cornwall.

You guys are my favorite! Please be okay!

I can't believe this is happening, I loved following your trip, I hope you're doing okay!

These two are such fakers. Does anyone really believe this?

I wonder if the police have checked to see if there are any submersibles in the area. Remember that one that went to go see the wreck of the Titanic? Maybe they're in something like that.

There were dozens more, each as unhelpful as the last. Harriet sighed and clicked back to the main page and watched a few more videos from their trip. She watched as they explored the town of Holyhead on the Welsh coast and tried to pronounce the words on the signs. *Creos i GYMRU*, announced one sign, with the English translation *Welcome to Wales* below it. *Ildiwich i gerbydau yn dod atoch*, said another sign, and the translation below it read *Yield to oncoming vehicles*. *Ysbyty* apparently directed people to the hospital. The Welsh people were fiercely proud of their language and cultural heritage, but Harriet was glad the signs also had English on them. Annie and Paul had fun pointing out the differences between the languages on the signs, and they also talked about the town on the Isle of Anglesey. It was a part of the country Harriet had never been to, and hoped to see someday.

After that, there was another video labeled *DISASTER! TOILET NEARLY BLEW UP!*

There was a short ad, and then they went on to describe in the video how, when they'd been docked at the last marina, they'd neglected to empty the tank that collected waste. The tank got full, and the toilet wouldn't flush any longer. It sounded horrible and smelly. But it didn't sound as though the toilet had nearly blown up. They simply emptied the tank at the next marina.

Harriet thought once again that the inflammatory headline seemed somewhat overblown for what actually happened—in this case, nothing—but their followers sure seemed to respond.

I'm so glad you're safe!
You guys! Be careful!
Please take care of yourselves!

Morons shouldn't be allowed to have a boat if they don't know how to use it.

Are you guys going to Scotland soon? I can't wait to see what you do there!

Harriet watched one more video, about a stop on the Isle of Man, an island in the Irish Sea between Ireland and Western Yorkshire. Then she looked at the clock. It was nearly time to go to the clinic. Her first appointment would be there soon. But she had a few minutes, and she wondered what she could find if she spent just a few minutes searching.

Paul Bellingham, she typed into the search engine. It wasn't such a common name that there was all that much to wade through. She found him pretty easily. The first thing that came up was the couple's webpage, where they talked about who they were and what they did and had links to their latest videos. There were links to email the couple, with one email address for fans and another for companies interested in sponsorship. There were also short bios of the couple. According to Paul's, he was born in Portsmouth, attended Oxford, where he'd studied engineering, then obtained a PhD at Yale and went on to work at some companies she'd heard of. It was an impressive résumé.

And even though Harriet hated herself for thinking it, she couldn't help but wonder... So why was he making videos about his toilet backing up for a living?

She navigated away from his website and clicked on the next link that came up, which was a link to a career-based social-media site. People posted their résumés there when they were looking for jobs or to share with professional connections. Harriet had her own profile on this site as a way to keep in touch with veterinarian colleagues around the world. Paul's profile was posted, and it listed nearly half a dozen jobs he'd performed, most of which weren't the same companies as those listed on his website. That didn't necessarily mean one or the other was untrue, but she noticed how short the duration at some of the companies was, and how often he seemed to change. Sure, people changed jobs for all kinds of reasons. Still, it seemed odd.

Then she clicked on a link that took her to a different social-media profile, one of the big ones, and she read a few of his posts. They were, in typical social-media style, mostly humble brags about cool places he'd been to or things he'd eaten or done. But she also found his name linked to a site that seemed to be some sort of neighborhood group, where in one post people complained about a neighbor who refused to clean up his yard on a street in a place called Tooting. Paul had posted repeatedly about this loud next-door neighbor for several months, and then his voice vanished from the discussion. Now that Harriet knew where his next-door neighbor lived, it only took a few seconds in an online search to discover the address where Paul had lived. It was a small, attached house in Tooting, which, as far as she could tell, was an area in Southern London. Not one of the fashionable neighborhoods she would have expected for this couple. That was interesting.

In a search bar, she typed in the address and found the house, owned by Paul and Annie Bellingham, had sold just a few months back. It had sold for much lower than she would have expected. The next link for the address was... Well, this was interesting.

It was a legal notice, published in the *South London Press*, announcing the foreclosure sale of the house in Tooting. And it was dated just a few months ago. They hadn't sold their house. It had been foreclosed on.

But that couldn't be right. They were wealthy. Annie had a trust fund. They had given up their jobs and were sailing around the UK, for goodness' sake. Surely they weren't the kind of people who got behind on a mortgage for a small terraced house in the suburbs?

But then again, this was hardly the first indication she'd gotten that they weren't everything they appeared to be. There were those comments about them being fakers. The lie about the upholstery. There was the bit about where the boat was registered. Had it really belonged to Annie's grandfather after all? There was the fact that the police no longer believed their story about being swept overboard and now suspected something else was going on.

The only real surprise was that Harriet hadn't seen it earlier. She'd believed—as, apparently, most of their fans had—that what they presented in their videos was the truth. But the more Harriet learned, the more she understood that not everything with Annie and Paul was as it seemed.

She typed *Annie Bellingham* into a search bar, but before she could hit return, a gray station wagon pulled into the parking area in front of the clinic. She needed to get going.

"You guys ready?" she said to Charlie and Maxwell. She opened the door to the clinic and ushered them through. Both the cat and dog scampered out of the kitchen, and Mercedes followed timidly.

"How about you, Ash?" she asked the kitten, who sat near the stove. He closed his eyes and turned his head away from her.

"Not today, huh?"

Harriet walked into the office and unlocked the front door. She got things set up just as Mrs. Scroggins came in with Winky in his cat carrier. Polly breezed in a few steps behind her, apologizing profusely.

"Van worked late last night, and I tried to go to bed, but I couldn't sleep until he got home, so then I was exhausted and slept through my alarm," Polly said in one long breath while she flopped down on her chair, turned on her computer, and smiled up at Mrs. Scroggins. "How is the little love bug doing?"

"Winky is great." Mrs. Scroggins didn't seem to know how else to respond to Polly's long-winded explanation, so she smiled awkwardly.

"You can bring him right on in," Harriet said, indicating Winky's cat carrier. She ushered the cat and his owner in and then spent the next few hours seeing patients. When they had a break for lunch, she walked to the waiting area to check in.

"Anything else before I go grab a sandwich?" she asked Polly.

"Yes," Polly said. "You got a call from Oliver down at the library. He says he found something about some ship captain he thought you'd want to see."

"He found something about the *Visiter*?"

"I don't know, but he seemed to think you'd want to know about it. He has it at the library for you."

"Thank you." Harriet did some quick math in her head. If she grabbed a sandwich, she'd have time to run down to the library before their afternoon appointments started. There was some research she wanted to do anyway.

"I can handle cleaning up the exam room. You go," Polly said. Harriet felt, far from the first time, grateful for having someone so capable working beside her.

"Thank you." Harriet decided to head to the library first—food could wait—and a few minutes later found Oliver at the front desk. He led her into the reference room and pulled out a book bound in dark blue linen. Its pages were a dark yellowish brown that suggested it was a very old book.

"This is an autobiography by Lord Archibald Beresford, an ancestor of the current Lord Beresford."

"I know Liam."

"Really?" Oliver lifted an eyebrow. She knew it was unusual for her to call the baron a friend, considering he was famously reclusive, but she didn't feel like explaining that right now. "Archibald was the younger brother of Liam Beresford's great-great-something grandfather, and he was something of a collector of, shall we say, unusual items."

"I've seen the collection up at the old manor house," Harriet told him. "If he's responsible for any of that, I know exactly what you mean." There was a room in Beresford Manor full of all kinds of odd antiquities—a stuffed jaguar, a portion of a marble column from Greece, a display of early bronze tools, an African ceremonial mask, a drapery-enclosed Louis XIV bed, an elephant's foot umbrella stand, a collection of pistols in a glass case, a grass skirt, gemstones in various stages of refinement, and a collection of Paleolithic skulls, among many other oddities.

Oliver lifted an eyebrow again but, showing typical British restraint, did not ask for more information about that.

"In his autobiography, Archibald spends some time lamenting the loss of items he'd been waiting for on a ship that went down near White Church Bay. He doesn't name the *Visiter* specifically, but he does talk about the loss of the items he was expecting." He held out the book, open to the page he wanted her to see. Harriet took it from him and read the section he indicated.

Trueman had, of course, being a local captain, supplied many of my favorite items over the years, and it was with great rejoicing that I learned he'd survived the ordeal. I was, however, deeply saddened to learn that several of the items that were procured for me from around the world went missing when his ship went down. The necklace was by far the most valuable, with sapphires straight from the heart of Africa, but it was the tortoise I was most saddened to lose. The creature was said to be quite fascinating. I was told it had been brought from its home in East Africa to India, where the son of an officer in the East India Company received the animal as a Christmas gift one year, no bigger than a pack of cards. The boy, James Merritt, loved the tortoise, but by the time his father was sent back to England, the animal was too big to take with them, and I was glad to secure him at a reasonable fee. The tortoise was loaded onto the Visiter, *but sadly no trace was ever found of it after the ship's passing. I was not the only one in the area who mourned the loss of goods on that ship, however, there are no doubt many in the area whose parties will be less raucous this winter than would have been had this tragedy not occurred.*

> *Trueman, it must be said, was completely distraught over not only the loss of the cargo but also of his ship. His whole fortune had been invested in the* Visiter, *and he was forced to rely on the charity of the Shipwrecked Mariner's Society to help recover from the tragedy before I stepped in and offered to invest in a new ship for his troubles. Some have claimed it was great generosity that motivated my actions, and I do not wish to dissuade anyone of that opinion, but it must also be said that there is none other so willing to procure goods from all four corners of the world for such a fine price.*

After that, Archibald went on to talk about the other generous gifts he'd given to those in the area over the years, and he moved away from the topic of the tortoise and the shipwreck. Harriet read the paragraphs over again, trying to make sense of them.

James Merritt. Did the boy who received the baby tortoise as a Christmas gift carve his initials in the tortoise's shell? It had to be, didn't it?

"So I guess we know why the tortoise was on board the ship," Harriet said. "And who its intended recipient was."

"It does sound like it was Archibald," Oliver said. "And it helps explain why there was a tortoise, as well as a sapphire necklace, a Japanese screen, and several barrels of whiskey on board a ship that was supposed to be carrying nothing but coal."

White Church Bay was well known for its history as a center for smuggling. Many of the fisherman's cottages and businesses were connected by underground tunnels so items could be brought in from ships and carried through the town without being spotted.

Harriet had been part of finding one of those tunnels just a few months before.

"Trueman's ship was registered in Whitby?" she asked.

"That's right."

"Huh."

"What do you mean, huh?"

Harriet was sure it was a longshot, but since she'd arrived in Yorkshire, she'd been made aware how many families had been here for hundreds of years. It wasn't just the gentry that passed houses and land down through the ages. Many of the farms and fisherman's cottages in town had been owned by the same families for generations.

"I'm just wondering if there are still any Robinsons around," she said. "And if they might know more about the goods that were on the ship when it went down. Any records, or anything like that."

"You mean, like whether there were any carvings in the shell of the tortoise?"

"It seems unlikely there was more than one giant tortoise in the area around that time, doesn't it?" Harriet said. "But it would be great to know for sure."

"There's a Peter Robinson in the village," Oliver said. "He lives in one of the fisherman's cottages, so I suppose it's possible, but I don't know if he's related."

Just then an older woman walked up to the reference desk and asked for help locating an old newspaper. Oliver excused himself, and Harriet thought for a moment about what to do next. She should probably head back to the clinic, but now that she thought about it, if she wanted to learn about the history and family of Trueman

Robinson, it might not be that hard. She could go to the cemetery and look at the headstones. Chances were good he was buried around these parts. Or she could search through old newspapers, looking for obituaries. But she had another idea.

She sat down at a computer and navigated the library's homepage to find the link that took her to the ancestry website. The library had a subscription to the service, which made it free for patrons to build their own family trees or to search those created by other people. There was no guarantee that Trueman Robinson would appear in any of the family trees on the site, but just in case…

Harriet found the search bar and typed the name *Trueman Robinson* in, and…there. She found a tree created by a Wilhemina Robinson, who appeared to be Trueman's great-great-granddaughter. That meant she was a first cousin of Peter Robinson, of White Church Bay. Which meant that Peter was a descendant of the famed captain.

Harriet didn't know Peter Robinson and had no idea how he would respond to her asking about his great-great-grandfather's extra-curricular shipping activities, but she figured it couldn't hurt to ask. She'd see if Will or Aunt Jinny knew him. That would be better than calling him out of the blue, she supposed. In any case, she had a plan of attack now.

While she was there, she decided to do a little more research into Annie and Paul Bellingham. First, she searched *property records UK*. In the US, property records were grouped by county, but she wasn't sure about how it was done in England's database. She quickly found that there was a government site that made it pretty easy, and she typed in the address she'd found for Annie and Paul in South

London. The information came up right away, along with recent sale prices. She shouldn't have been surprised to see that it had sold for far less than what they'd paid for it, not since she already knew it had been foreclosed on, but it was still interesting to see.

Then she navigated to a different government website, one that listed the names of everyone who had filed for bankruptcy in the past five years in the UK. If the Bellinghams had lost their house, there was a decent chance they had also filed for bankruptcy. She entered the name *Paul Bellingham* and, sure enough, his name was listed.

But what did that tell her? That they had money trouble, sure. That there was some credibility to the comments that suggested Annie and Paul were lying, or "fakes." They'd certainly lied about at least a good chunk of their public life. Harriet wondered what else they'd lied about. Did Annie really have a trust fund? Had Paul actually gone to Oxford or Yale?

She didn't know how to look into financial records, but she decided to start with a simple internet search. Looking for *Annie Bellingham* turned up a wedding announcement in *The London Times*. Harriet read it carefully. It said Annie had gone to the Royal College of Art in London, and Paul to Oxford and Yale. It said they lived in London and that he worked in finance and she worked at a gallery. It said that Annie's maiden name was Young and that she was the daughter of Ernest and Virginia Young, of London.

Harriet searched for the name Ernest Young, and... Well, this was interesting.

CHAPTER TEN

A search for the name Ernest Young pretty quickly turned up some dismal stories. Ernest had inherited great wealth, according to an article in the *Financial Times*, and had a successful career in banking. He lived in the family's home in Mayfair, one of the wealthiest neighborhoods in London. But according to this article, Ernest was one of several very wealthy people whose fortunes were lost when a risky financial investment was revealed to be a scam. A Ponzi scheme. It had been all over the news, and many famous people were taken in. The family, according to the article, had lost everything, including the home in Mayfair and all their investments.

So. Annie's family had been posh, it seemed. She wasn't lying about that. But their fortunes had changed when their investments imploded.

Harriet thought for a moment. How could she find out about Paul? She didn't know how to check Oxford's enrollment records, but she could probably find out whether he'd ever enrolled in Yale. The historic college was only a couple hours' drive from where she had grown up in Connecticut, and her ex-fiancé, Dustin, had attended Yale for his undergraduate degree. She knew from her time with him that there was a strong alumni network, including an online directory where an alum could search for the contact information of other alums. If Paul had gone to Yale, Dustin would be able to find him. A year ago, she wouldn't have dared reach out to him, but he'd come to see her in the spring, shortly before she'd gotten engaged to Will, and they'd cleared the air. He was dating someone who seemed wonderful, Harriet was happy with Will, and they'd texted back and forth a few times in recent months. He'd congratulated her on her wedding. It wouldn't be weird if she reached out to him now to ask for his help.

Can I ask you for a favor? I'm trying to find out whether someone who claims they went to Yale actually did, she texted him.

Easy enough to verify. What's the name?

Paul Bellingham.

Any idea what year?

Not sure what year. Grad school.

Let me check.

Harriet really needed to get going. She logged out of the websites and databases she'd used, and it was less than two minutes later that Dustin got back to her.

There's no one by that name in the alumni directory. If he went here, he opted out of a listing. But no one opts out of the directory, so pretty sure he didn't go here.

Thank you, she texted. I appreciate it.

No problem. Hope you're doing well.

She needed to call Van to let him know what she'd learned. But she was already running late. She would call him later. She packed up and headed back to the clinic, stopping only briefly at home to scarf down a ham and cheese sandwich. Then she made a quick call before greeting their first patient of the afternoon.

"Hi, Aunt Jinny," she said when her aunt answered. "How are you?"

"Good. You caught me between appointments. What's going on?"

"Do you know someone named Peter Robinson who lives in the village?"

"Sure. Peter's a great guy. Used to play golf with your uncle Dom. Recently retired, I believe. Why?"

"It seems he's a descendant of the *Visiter*'s captain."

"Yes, I suppose that would make sense. His family has been here for quite a while."

"I was wondering if you might be able to introduce me to him."

"Of course. I'll give him a call this afternoon."

"Thank you."

That afternoon Harriet vaccinated a bulldog, prescribed medicine for digestion issues in a parakeet, and drew a blood sample from an elderly golden retriever. Before she knew it, it was closing time. Polly swept and mopped, and they were ready to leave just as Van pulled up in front.

At least this would save her a call. She smiled when Van walked in, and said, "Any news on the boaters?"

"I'm afraid not," Van said, grimacing. "There's still no sign of them. Which would be a major reason to worry if we thought they were actually in danger."

"What about that boat registration? Any luck on that?"

Van sighed. "Okay, look, this isn't public information, but I can tell you that the boat was indeed not registered in Plymouth. Not only that, it wasn't even registered to the Bellinghams."

"What?" Polly's eyebrows disappeared under her bangs. "Who is it registered to, then?"

"Some bloke in Hull. Says he sold them the boat back in July, but apparently, he should have waited for the check to clear before turning over the keys. He claims he never got paid for it. He was waiting to transfer the title and registration until he got the money, but he never got it. So the boat is still registered in his name."

"So it's definitely not her grandfather's boat," Harriet said.

"Definitely not."

"He must be really upset," Harriet said. "They have his boat, and he's out thousands of pounds."

"Many thousands of pounds," Polly added. "I don't know how much a boat like that would cost, but it has to be a lot."

"'A lot' is an understatement," Van said.

"So you're saying that not only are they *not* lost at sea, they were sailing around the UK in a stolen sailboat?" Polly shook her head.

"What's his name?" Harriet asked. Maybe she would do some looking into him. "The guy who technically still owns the boat?"

"Don't think I can tell you that," Van said, shaking his head. "Sorry, Harriet. I've already told you all I can."

"I understand," Harriet said. "I was doing some research today, and I found a few things I thought were interesting."

"What kind of things?" Van asked.

"Polly, you told me some people call Annie and Paul fake, and I couldn't figure out why."

"They're just jealous," Polly said. "It's because they're posh, and people are wishing they had the things Annie and Paul have."

"Like their grandfather's sailboat?" Van raised an eyebrow.

Polly rolled her eyes.

"I don't doubt that there are plenty of people like that out there," Harriet said. "But I did some digging, and I discovered that the internet trolls may be right. Annie and Paul lived in London, correct?"

"Yeah. In her family's house in Mayfair."

"Actually, Annie grew up in Mayfair, but the family lost the house when she was a child, after her father's fortune evaporated when a hedge fund that paid ridiculous returns went under."

"Yes, we know about that," Van said.

Polly blinked, clearly trying to make sense of this. "But the house in their videos—the one they lived in?"

"It's certainly not her family's house. They actually lived at one time in a terraced house in Tooting, which was foreclosed on earlier this year."

"In *Tooting*?" Polly's mouth hung open. "For real?"

"That's right," Van said. "The couple filed for bankruptcy themselves shortly before the house was repossessed. This is all public knowledge," he added, when Polly looked at him questioningly.

"So the haters were right?" Polly was clearly having a hard time processing this.

"And get this," Harriet said. "Paul's résumé says he went to Oxford and then graduate school at Yale. But I checked with an alum I know, and there's no record of Paul in the alumni directory there."

"Huh." Van shifted on his feet and started writing in a small notepad. "This is something we didn't know," he said.

"Maybe he started at the school, but never finished?" Polly suggested.

"His online résumé says he graduated with a master's degree, so he's not telling the truth somewhere," Harriet said.

Van made furious notes. "We'll look into that."

"I can't believe the haters were right," Polly said. "I believed Annie and Paul."

"Someone obviously knew they weren't representing themselves accurately," Harriet said. "I think the real question is, who knew it, and how? And did that person have anything to do with whatever happened to Annie and Paul?"

"Blimey," Polly said under her breath. "You'll look into that, won't you, Van?"

"Yes, we'll look into it," Van said, still scribbling in his notepad.

Just then his phone beeped. He set the notebook down and pulled the phone out of his pocket.

"Polly, I have to go."

"What is it? What happened?"

"I'm sorry, I have to run. Is there any chance—"

"I can give her a ride home," Harriet said. "What's going on?"

Harriet hadn't actually expected Van to tell her, but maybe because of the excitement of the moment, or because of the tip about Paul's résumé she'd given him, he answered her.

"Annie's cell phone just pinged a cell tower in Whitby," he said. "They're nearby."

CHAPTER ELEVEN

Harriet wanted desperately to follow Van to wherever he was headed to find out more about the signal that had pinged the cell tower. But she knew she would never be allowed to tag along, so instead she let the animals into the house and told them she'd be back after she drove Polly home.

"Thanks for the ride," Polly said as they pulled out of the parking lot. "I knew before I married Van that his job is unpredictable, but knowing it is different from experiencing it. He's always rushing off to work on cases, even when he's supposed to be off."

"That's got to be tough," Harriet said. She understood—in the few weeks she and Will had been married, he'd already had to dash off a couple of times when an emergency cropped up with his flock.

"We were supposed to order in curry and watch the Arsenal game he didn't get to see yesterday because he was working." She sighed. "Now he'll probably be working till who knows when. I still want that curry though."

"You should order it anyway and watch whatever you want."

"*Gilmore Girls* it is."

Harriet laughed. Polly had recently begun rewatching the family drama from the early two thousands. "I don't know why you're suddenly so obsessed with that show."

"Because it's a good one," Polly said. "And because I'm convinced you grew up in Stars Hollow."

"I didn't grow up in Stars Hollow," Harriet said, laughing about the idealized New England town that was a central character on the show. "It's a fictional place."

"I don't believe you. Anyway, Rory is in her 'Jess' phase, and everyone knows Jess is the best boyfriend, so I'll have a good night, even without Van." She sighed again. "It's weird, trying to figure out how to live with someone else, isn't it? Like, I spent most of my life doing what I pleased, and now I can't do that. There's this whole other person whose life is connected to mine. And he has a wildly unpredictable schedule, which I guess is something I'm going to have to get used to, but it isn't exactly as smooth as everyone always makes it seem, right?"

She looked over at Harriet hopefully.

"Or, wait, you and Will are so perfect for each other you probably don't even know what I'm talking about."

"No, I definitely do," Harriet said. She tried to choose her words carefully. She wanted to commiserate with Polly while still respecting Will and their relationship. "I love Will, and I couldn't be happier that I get to live with him and spend my life with him. But is it always easy? Of course not. We've only been married a few weeks, so it's not exactly the same situation as you and Van, but yeah, we're definitely getting used to living together and what that looks like. We've both been on our own for a long time, and we're used to doing things our own way. We're trying to figure out what it will look like to do them together."

She flipped on her blinker and turned onto a side street. "And," she added as she slowed to let a man walking a dog cross the road,

"Will's schedule is unpredictable too. He left before dawn today to visit a parishioner in the hospital. On the one day I didn't have an early morning appointment and I could've slept in. I'm trying to get used to it, since I know that's always going to be a part of his job."

"It's hard to get used to it though," Polly said. "When the job comes first, again and again. I mean, I know what Van does is important, and it's not like he's leaving me hanging because he wants to. He's out there trying to save lives, so it's awful for me to even be complaining about it."

"It's not awful," Harriet said. "It's totally normal for you to feel upset about it, even if you do recognize how important his job is. I'll admit I wasn't too happy when Will got the call at four a.m. that he was needed at a dying man's bedside. But what could I do? Get mad that someone had a crisis and needed their minister and the timing wasn't convenient for me?" She shrugged. "But honestly, I kind of wanted to. I knew what I signed up for when I married a minister, but that doesn't mean it's easy when his job interrupts our life."

"Right," Polly said, nodding. "Because for both Van and for Will, it's not just a job, it's a calling. Which is great. But it's also easy to feel like second fiddle behind the job."

"Luckily, we both married really great guys, and if the worst thing we have to deal with is them being out there saving the world, I suppose we can handle that," Harriet said.

"I guess so." Polly blew out a breath. "I'm getting the kind of curry I like though. Extra spicy."

"You do you," Harriet said, laughing as she drove up in front of the small apartment building where Polly and Van lived. "Have a good night."

"You too," Polly said, opening her car door. "What are you up to tonight, then? A nice quiet evening alone with your handsome hubby?"

"Thank goodness, yes," Harriet said. After leaving the house so early, he'd probably be home by now, and hopefully had the water boiling. "It's been a crazy few days, and I just need Will and a giant bowl of pasta."

"Sounds like heaven." Polly climbed out, slung her bag over her shoulder, and waved as she headed for the door. Harriet turned the car around and looked both ways, but just before she pulled out into the road, her phone rang.

Will.

"Hey. I was just chatting with Polly about you," Harriet said.

"Oh yeah? All good, I hope?"

"I was saying how lucky I am to be married to you."

"Oh good. I was talking about you a few minutes ago, telling Eli how good your cooking is. He wasn't doing anything, so I invited him over to try it himself."

Eli. That was the Coastguard guy. "That sounds good. When did you invite him over for?" They had plans on Saturday, but they could probably make Friday work, if they got the shopping and the housecleaning done.

"Tonight. We're headed to the house now."

"Tonight?!"

"Yeah, I figured I should give you a heads-up instead of showing up with Eli in tow."

"Will, the house is a mess. I'm a mess. We don't have any food for company. I was just going to make pasta."

"Pasta is great. I love pasta."

"I love pasta too," called a voice on his end of the line. Wonderful. Eli was listening to the whole conversation.

"Is this—" Will faltered. "You don't sound happy about this."

"I'm not—" She couldn't have this conversation now, not if Eli was there listening.

"It's fine," she said. She saw her hopes for a nice quiet evening with Will evaporate.

"Are you sure?"

What could she say? They were already on their way. The conversation about when and how to invite guests over would have to wait for another time.

"I'll see you guys soon."

When Harriet got home, she put a pot of water on to boil, and then she flew around the main floor, picking up stray pieces of clothing, stacking the mail in a pile, wiping the counters. She found some parmesan in the fridge and a little bit of pecorino-Romano cheese from a basket someone had given them as a wedding present. She had spaghetti noodles and pepper. *Cacio e pepe*, then. By the time Will's and Eli's cars pulled into the driveway, the house was at least presentable, though certainly not as clean as she would have wanted for having guests over.

"Hi, sweetheart," Will said, bending forward to kiss her after she answered the door. "You remember Eli?"

"Nice to see you again," she said, reaching out her hand. Eli was tall and lanky, with close-cropped brown hair and freckles splashed across his nose.

"It's great to see you, Mrs. Knight. Thanks so much for having me." He bent down to pet Maxwell and Mercedes, who had both rushed to the door.

"Of course. And please, call me Harriet."

"All right. Harriet. And it's good to see you again," he said to Mercedes. "She's looking much better than when I saw her last."

"She was hungry and scared then, but she seems to be doing all right here." She ushered him in and offered him a drink. Once he was seated on a counter barstool with a glass of soda, she turned to Will, who was washing a rather sad-looking head of lettuce. "So, did you two run into each other today?"

"Oh, no," Will said. "Eli is part of the small group I lead at the Coastguard base."

Right. She'd forgotten that Will was a chaplain at the Whitby station. She began to grate the parmesan.

"He's at the base a lot," Eli said, "so he's more like an honorary member of the team than our pastor."

"Sometimes they even let me go with them on drills," Will said with a grin.

"They do?" It was hard to believe they would let a civilian tag along when they chased down pirates or arrested smugglers.

"Only the routine stuff," Eli said with a smile. "Don't worry, he's not in any danger."

"That's true," Will said. "You always think the Coastguard is all about dramatic sea rescues, but really, it's almost entirely about customs and border enforcement. Making sure no one is smuggling goods or people in or out of the country."

"Though, truthfully, sometimes civilians help us out with that stuff," Eli said, tipping an imaginary hat to Harriet. "And we're grateful."

Eli was a nice young man, and she felt her frustration beginning to melt away as they chatted. It certainly wasn't his fault Will had invited him over with no notice, so she would just focus on getting to know him and making him feel welcome, and she'd talk to Will about it later.

"After Bible study, I asked Eli about how the search was going for the Bellinghams, and he told me something interesting," Will said. "I thought you'd want to hear it too."

"Oh?" Was that what Will had been thinking, asking him here? Or was that Will saying that now, trying to get back in her good graces? "What's that?" Satisfied with her pile of parmesan, she started grating the pecorino-Romano.

"We've got the sailboat tied up at our dock in the marina. Since the police processed it, it's just been there, waiting for the owners or whatever is going to happen with it."

"Has there been any sign of the missing sailors?" Harriet asked.

"As of today, we've officially called off the search," Eli said. "We've been out there looking for them with boats and helicopters every day since Sunday, and there's been no trace of them. Captain Scully finally called the search off because, frankly, the chances are very slim of finding them alive if they're out there on the ocean. We hate to give up, but at some point, it becomes necessary."

"Will and I have been thinking that they might not have gone overboard in the storm," Harriet said. "We think something else happened to them."

"Well, right, there's that too," Eli said. "We kept with the search, just in case, but that's over as of today. But also today, someone showed up at the marina. This guy came into the station, demanding we turn the sailboat over to him, saying it's his boat. Captain Scully calmed him down and got the story out of him. He says he sold the Bellinghams the boat but they never paid him, or the check bounced, or something."

"The guy from Hull? He came to Whitby?" Harriet said.

"Yep. Anthony Maglione," Eli said.

Anthony Maglione. She filed that name away.

"Do you think he had anything to do with their disappearance?" Harriet asked.

"We don't know yet, though of course we're going to check. We're also looking to see if he shows up on any of the message boards we monitor. You'd be surprised how bold people are on some public threads, assuming no one will know who they are. We're watching a few threads where people talk about boating on this part of the coast specifically, and there's stuff that's not always aboveboard."

"Nice one." Will grinned at Eli, and it took Harriet a moment to realize their guest had made a boating pun. Eli grinned back at Will and then kept talking.

"If he's ever commented on one of the message boards, it shouldn't be hard to connect him. But so far, that's just a theory. When he showed up, he said he saw the article in the paper this morning and was quite upset. He kept insisting the boat is his. Yelling about how he was going to sue us if we didn't release the boat."

"Are you sure he's British? Sounds like an American to me." Will looked at Harriet with a wry grin.

She laughed. She knew Will was teasing her to try to get her to relax. The annoying thing was that it was working.

Eli grinned. "Apparently, he filed a report with the police in Hull last week, claiming he knew who had his boat. I never got the full story out of him, but that was something exciting I wasn't expecting today."

"Will you release the boat to him?" Will asked.

"We won't be releasing the boat to anyone until we know what's what," Eli said.

But Harriet thought about something else she'd learned. "You said this Anthony person was in Whitby today?"

"Boy, was he ever. He first went down to the marina and barked at the guys on the dock, then made his way up to the station."

Harriet knew roughly where the station was, a few streets from the river Esk, in the steep hills of Whitby. But that wasn't what she was focused on.

"Do you know when this was? Like, was it this morning, or—"

"It was this afternoon," Eli said. "Not long before Bible study started. Why?"

"Annie's and Paul's phones have been missing, right?" Harriet asked.

"That's what I was told," Eli said, nodding.

"Wherever they are, they've been kept off, with location tracking off," Will said.

"Well, I was told that, late this afternoon, one of their phones pinged a cell tower in Whitby," Harriet said. "At first I assumed that meant they were in the area somewhere, but now I'm wondering…"

"If Anthony has their phones?" Will said.

"Right." The water was boiling, so she tossed in the spaghetti and stirred it with a wooden spoon. "Is there any way this Anthony person could have Annie's and Paul's phones?"

"But how would he have gotten them?" Eli asked.

"I suppose the only logical conclusion was that he took them," Harriet said.

"Took them when?" Will asked, though she was pretty sure he was thinking the same thing she was.

Harriet looked at Eli. "You said he was upset when he was there today, right?"

"Very much so," Eli said.

"He said Annie and Paul stole the boat from him, right?" She set the spoon on the counter and pulled out the pepper grinder.

"That's right," Eli said.

"If they didn't get swept overboard," Harriet said, "that leaves only two possibilities. One, they left the boat on their own for some reason, and left it floating on the water, or two, they were removed from the boat against their will."

"And you think Anthony could have been upset enough about the boat to remove them?" Eli asked.

"I don't know," Harriet said. "But it's a question worth considering, for sure."

"He had to find them first," Will said. "Let's assume he tracked them down before they turned off their AIS signal and he followed them along the coast."

"Okay." Harriet nodded. "So he boards the boat, tosses them overboard, or whatever he does—" It felt callous to describe something so horrific so blandly, but she tried not to get bogged down in that for now. "So why doesn't he take his boat after that? Why did he leave it there?"

"Maybe something went wrong," Will said. "Things didn't go according to plan."

"Maybe he didn't intend to really hurt them," Eli suggested. "But the confrontation goes sideways, and he runs. Takes their phones, with all possible ways of tracking them turned off, and then he leaves the boat behind and makes a break for it. He realizes that the boat is now a crime scene, his DNA is all over it, and he decides his freedom is worth more than the boat. He leaves it behind and runs away."

"Would he really do all that over a sailboat?" Harriet asked, trying to make sense of it.

"This is not a little dinghy we're talking about," Eli said. "That boat is worth over a hundred thousand pounds. People have killed for far less."

Harriet gulped. They'd all been thinking it, but it was the first time anyone had said the words out loud. She set the knife down and thought through the scenario. There were still a couple of problems with it.

"But we were on the boat. It was messy, but it didn't look like a crime scene. There was no blood anywhere, or anything like that," she said.

"He cleaned up the blood," Eli said. "We couldn't see it, but an infrared camera would pick it up."

"And if he was worried about his DNA being found on the boat, why wouldn't he actually take the boat with him, so the police wouldn't find it?" Harriet asked.

"Because he knew Paul and Annie were going to be reported missing at some point. They're all over the internet in that boat," Eli said. "If he was found in possession of it, it'd be curtains for him."

Harriet thought for a moment then said, "But it doesn't really fit, does it? Why would he show up now, announcing that he's the owner of the boat and demanding it back? It doesn't make sense. If he really hurt them, or worse, why would he put himself squarely on the radar of the authorities by showing up at their doorstep?"

Will and Eli were quiet now, clearly trying to come up with answers to her objections.

"There's got to be something we're missing," Eli said. "Some clue that we don't have access to."

"Or else we're totally off base, and he has nothing to do with it," Harriet said. But even as she said it, she didn't believe it. It was too much of a coincidence that one of the cell phones was turned on at the same time this Anthony character showed up in Whitby.

"In any case, I'm sure the police are looking into it," Will said. "They'll be able to figure out where the mobile could have been, based on which cell tower it pinged, and trace Anthony's whereabouts in recent days. I'm sure they'll question him, if they haven't already." He was trying to move past this gruesome topic, Harriet knew, and as much as she wanted to keep coming up with theories, she suspected it was probably best to move the conversation along after all.

"Looks like the pasta's about done," she said. "Are you guys ready to eat?"

But just because they stopped talking about it didn't mean she stopped thinking about it. She needed to learn more about this Anthony guy.

CHAPTER TWELVE

Eli turned out to be a really great guy, and they had a nice dinner. Harriet learned he was from Edinburgh, and as Will's family was from Muckle Roe, he and Will brought out their best Scottish brogues and talked at length about the most beautiful parts of the Highlands.

"You've got to come to Scotland sometime," Eli said, in an assumed accent so thick she could hardly understand what he said. "Most beautiful place in the world, it is."

"Edinburgh is a gorgeous city," Will said in his best brogue. Though both of his parents were Scottish, Will had spent most of his life in Yorkshire, so his attempt at a Scottish accent fell quite a bit short of Eli's. "I'll take ye there someday."

"Aye, you've got to take your bride to your homeland, show her the place your people come from," Eli said.

Harriet wanted to make a joke about seeing Will in a skirt, but she'd learned early on in their relationship that kilts were no joke. Scots took their native dress very seriously. Bagpipes were also off-limits for humor.

They also talked about Eli's family, his border collie, Marcie, and what he liked most about his job. He had a girlfriend back home in Edinburgh, and he ran marathons in his spare time. Harriet couldn't deny that he was interesting and easy to talk to, and when he left, she meant it when she said she hoped he'd come again.

But that didn't mean she meant it any less when she closed the door, turned to Will, and said, "Please don't invite somebody over with no warning again."

"I'm sorry," Will said. "I could tell that upset you, and I promise I didn't mean to stress you out. It's just, I invite people over all the time, and it never occurred to me that you wouldn't be happy about it. I can see I was wrong about that, and I'm sorry."

The way he said it, she felt like a jerk for making a big deal about it. She could see that he genuinely hadn't known it would make her anxious and that he was struggling to understand why it had upset her.

"It's okay," she said. "I love that you love people. But when I'm having guests, I like to have a chance to plan a menu, to make something good, to clean the house up. I had to shove a pile of laundry in the hall closet because I didn't have time to take it upstairs."

"But no one cares about that kind of stuff," Will said. "When you invite someone into your home, they don't come because they want to eat a gourmet meal or see a spotless house. They come to talk with you and enjoy good company. I don't think you should worry about having a perfect home or a great meal. No one is judging you about those things. A grilled cheese sandwich or soup from a can is fine, with the right company."

Harriet shook her head. "My concern isn't about what other people think, believe it or not. It's about making a guest feel welcome in our home. When someone has taken the time to plan a menu they know you'll like, when they've cleared the clutter off their counter and made it seem like they care about your visit, it makes a big difference. For me, hospitality is about making someone feel special, like you care enough about them to put some thought into their visit."

"But people don't really care about those things. They care about being with you," Will said. "And when you invite someone over, even without two weeks' notice and a grocery run, it says 'I care about making time for you.' People feel seen. They don't care if you serve them crackers and a leftover hot dog, as long as you listen to them and get to know them."

Harriet could see that they held two very different versions of hospitality, and as frustrating as the conversation was, she tried to keep her cool.

"Maybe." That was as far as she was willing to go at the moment. "But *I* don't like it, Will," she said. "I had a long day at work and looked forward to getting off my feet and spending time with you, and suddenly I was trying to throw together a meal and make the house presentable." She took a deep breath and let it out slowly. "Like I said, I love that you love people and want to spend more time with them. But I would appreciate it if you would give me more notice next time."

Will stepped forward and took her hands. "I'm sorry. I'm used to being on my own, I guess. I'm not used to having to check in with someone about my every move."

Harriet opened her mouth, about to spit out some angry words, but Will held up his hand and said, "That came out wrong. What I meant was that I'm not used to putting someone else's feelings above my own, which is what I'm called to do in our marriage. I'm asking you to please be patient with me. I'm trying, Harriet, and I want nothing more than to make you happy. I love you. It's just going to take me some time to figure out how to do that. Will you please forgive me for tonight?"

Once more, Harriet felt like a heel. He hadn't meant to drive her crazy. He'd been a bachelor for most of his life, and an outgoing one at that, and had no doubt spent most of his life inviting parishioners over for dinner with no plan and no food. They probably thought it was charming that he was helpless in the kitchen and that he served them whatever he had on hand. That clueless, eternal optimism was what she'd fallen in love with, after all.

"Of course I forgive you," she said, leaning forward to plant a kiss on his lips. "I love you. We'll figure this out together."

That night, when Harriet kissed him good night, she couldn't help but think that if a little cluelessness and care for others was Will's worst trait, she was still incredibly blessed.

🐾 🐾

Harriet woke up in the middle of the night and couldn't go back to sleep, no matter how hard she tried. Her mind swirled with thoughts about Will, about Jim the tortoise, about the missing boaters.

She wondered why Annie and Paul had misrepresented themselves in their videos. Was there any chance they were in Whitby somewhere? Why would they be there—and where in Whitby would they be? Were they being held against their will? Were there really pirates? Even alien abduction didn't seem so far-fetched at three o'clock in the morning.

But also, she couldn't help but fixate on this Anthony Maglione person. Did he truly have something to do with Annie and Paul's disappearance? If they hadn't paid for the boat he sold them, it did give him a strong reason to confront them. Eli said Anthony was very angry when he'd come to the Coastguard station. Angry enough to lose his temper when he'd tracked them down? But how had they managed to sail off in a boat worth at least a hundred thousand pounds without paying for it?

Harriet pushed herself up quietly. Will rolled over, and Ash, sleeping by his side, adjusted his position. She got out of bed and padded down the stairs. She headed to the kitchen, warmed up a mug of milk, and then opened her laptop and pulled up a search window.

She typed in *Anthony Maglione* and scanned the results that came up. There were far too many, so she added the word *Hull* and searched again. Aha. There. This time the top result was a picture and biography on the website of a medical practice. It showed a mostly bald man with a ring of dark hair rimming his head, and big glasses. Anthony was a cardiologist and had been practicing in Hull for over two decades. That explained how he'd been able to afford a boat. He had attended medical school at the University of Sheffield and completed residencies at several hospitals before moving to Hull and starting his own practice. He had a wife and two grown daughters, and in his spare time he loved to garden, sail, and play the cello.

He sounded perfectly lovely. Then again, he wouldn't have put "sometimes flies into a murderous rampage" in his online bio, now would he? She had to keep digging.

She found an article in *The Hull Times* that featured his house in a holiday homes tour. He lived in a neighborhood of large brick Victorian homes surrounded by greenery and fountains, and apparently last year several of the finest homes had opened their doors to the public, including Anthony and Jessica Maglione. It was a beautiful three-story home, judging by the exterior, which was redbrick with Tudor-style beams on the front. The newspaper identified it as 8 Salisbury Street, just across the street from another home on the tour at 11 Salisbury Street, which was similar in style but larger. It looked like a nice neighborhood, and opening his home to others reinforced her idea that Anthony seemed like a decent guy. But appearances could be deceiving.

She also found links to a page where he was listed as a member of a team of volunteers who had gone to rural Kenya to treat people who needed medical attention. There was another page with several photos of the *Salacia*, one of which showed him proudly standing on the deck. It was the same boat, clearly. So what happened? Did this man have something to do with Annie and Paul's disappearance? She would need to find out more. An idea began forming in her mind. It was kind of crazy, so she'd have to think about it, but maybe.

In the meantime, she thought about something Eli had said at dinner that night. The Coastguard was monitoring message boards known for not really being "aboveboard." Message boards that discussed boating around their coast specifically. Could she find those too?

What would she even search for? She decided to be very direct and typed in *message board Whitby boat* and hit return. A number of threads popped up, and she skimmed through them, but they tended to mostly be about navigating the harbor and tie-up rules and fees.

There didn't seem to be anything there, so she went back to her results page. Farther down, she found a link to a message board she'd heard Polly talk about. It was a site where people discussed such subjects as the legal limit for how many lobsters a fisherman could capture per day and strategies to get away with bringing in more. That wasn't what she was looking for, but it was in the right ballpark. She clicked on the link and searched specifically for White Church Bay and Whitby. Just when she was about to give up and click the back arrow, she came across a thread where people seemed to be asking for favors from other fishermen.

One person called FishGuy asked if anyone had a tool for unblocking a clog in the head. She was pretty sure the "head" on a boat was a toilet. No thank you. Another person called BigMouth75 asked if anyone could help him get ahold of a commercial license without going through all the hoops. There were several replies to this one, some outraged at the idea, but also several people who replied that they would be messaging BigMouth privately. The people who intended to message BigMouth used unidentifiable names too, like GigglePop!, NarwhalLover43, and MeatHead713. She kept scrolling down the message board, not quite sure what she was looking for.

Wait. Here was something interesting. She took a long sip of her milk and studied the screen. Someone named Neptune posted a message one week ago that said, *I have a unique errand I'm looking for help with. I will make it worth your while. Any interest, message me privately to learn more.*

That could be anything. It could be totally innocuous. Or it could be completely relevant. The timing was what made her curious. It wasn't the most recent post on the page, but it was recent enough, just a few days before the boaters went missing. She looked at the responses and saw that TottenhamFan13 had left a comment making fun of the vagueness of the post, SharkSkin asked how much they were offering, a query that was never publicly answered, and someone called Nessie left a comment saying they were sending a private message.

She clicked on SharkSkin's name and was taken to the posts they had authored or commented on. On the one asking about skirting lobster limits, they said it was easy to hide live lobsters in the head of your boat if anyone boarded to search. The toilet again. They had also replied to someone asking whether it was possible to enter or leave Whitby Harbor without getting picked up by security cameras. SharkSkin replied, *Sadly, not in my experience. There are cameras all over the marina, especially at the entrance. If you need to go in or out unnoticed, try doctoring the reg number on your hull. That way the cameras will pick up the wrong number and send them on a wild-goose chase.*

Goodness. What were these people doing that they needed to go unnoticed? And it was startling how casually this person had suggested changing the registration number on a boat. That was a crime, she was pretty sure. But there were no posts that told her if this person was actually involved in what had happened to Annie and Paul.

She went back and looked at the comments and posts left by Nessie. A year ago, Nessie answered a question about where to find cheap life vests that looked real enough to pass Coastguard inspection. There was another question about where to find cheap parts to make repairs. That advice, from eighteen months ago, was to go to the boat storage areas of the marina and to take parts from the boats stored there over the winter. *The summer people won't notice until June, and they're clearly rich enough to be able to afford replacement parts*, Nessie promised.

That was disheartening. But all of it make her think that maybe she wasn't too far off base, thinking someone on this message board might be involved with whatever happened to Annie and Paul. She wondered what Nessie had written privately to Neptune and whether any of it had anything do with the missing couple.

She decided to see if she could figure out who was behind the name Nessie. It might be short for a longer name—maybe Vanessa? She ran a search for the name Vanessa on the site, and when that didn't turn up anything, for the name Vanessa in Whitby and White Church Bay. She found an eighty-two-year-old grandmother in Ravenscar who kept chickens and embroidered Bible verses onto pillows. Probably not her.

She turned when she heard footsteps coming down the stairs.

"You okay?" Will asked. His hair was mussed, and he blinked against the kitchen light.

"I couldn't sleep," Harriet said. "Sorry if I woke you up."

"You didn't," Will said. "But when I woke up and you weren't there, I got worried."

"I'm all right. I just can't get my mind to settle down."

"Come back to bed." He reached out to take her hand.

Harriet considered whether she'd be able to fall asleep. The milk helped some, but her mind still raced.

Will glanced at her screen. "Nessie?"

"It's a long story. I'm trying to find someone around here who goes by that name."

"You should probably aim about five hundred kilometers north."

"What?"

"Nessie? As in the Loch Ness Monster?"

Harriet groaned. How had she not made that connection?

"Oh wow. I've just spent fifteen minutes trying to find someone named Nessie."

"It if makes you feel any better, people have spent hundreds of years trying to find the Loch Ness Monster."

"I can't believe it."

"Believe it. There are many stories about people seeing a giant sea monster in the lake, but several reputable scientific explorations haven't turned up anything. If you take the boat tour of the loch, they basically tell you it's just a large eel."

"I don't mean that," she said with a laugh. "I can't believe I didn't make the connection. It's so obvious."

"Aye, I guess you needed a Scotsman to point it out to ye," he said, bringing back his brogue.

"Why would someone choose that as their screen name?" Harriet asked.

Will shrugged. "Maybe they're Scottish. Maybe they're a sea monster. Maybe there's no reason at all. Come to bed, and we'll figure it out in the morning."

He took her hand. Reluctantly, she closed the laptop and followed him up the stairs.

CHAPTER THIRTEEN

Harriet woke to the smell of coffee brewing and bacon frying. She rolled over and found Ash sleeping on Will's pillow. She reached out to scratch the kitten on his soft little head, but he hissed when she got close. Not today, then. She would win him over eventually though. She pushed herself out of bed, and after wrapping a robe around herself, she padded down the stairs and into the kitchen.

"Something smells good," she said.

"Did you get back to sleep all right? I made you coffee." Will reached for the coffeepot. He poured a stream into the cup, and she could already tell it was far too weak, but she took the cup gratefully. He had a cup of milky tea with a Yorkshire Gold teabag resting on the saucer waiting for himself.

"Thank you." She added milk and sugar and took a long sip. There was a plate with a stack of waffles on the table, and maple syrup was heating in a saucepan on the stove. "What motivated you to make a breakfast feast?"

"I don't have any meetings until ten today, and I wanted to let my beautiful wife know how much I love her," he said, using a fork to pry the last of the strips of bacon off the pan and onto a plate. "So I made a special breakfast for you. Bon appétit."

"This smells wonderful." Harriet actually had to run. She had a horse with an intestinal illness she was due to check out in half an hour, and the farm was fifteen minutes away. But she couldn't exactly run out on Will now, not after all the effort he'd put in for her.

They sat down at the table, and Will prayed over the food. As they ate, he chatted about a choir rehearsal that afternoon and a baptism that was coming up, and Harriet was grateful all over again for her adorable, loving, kind husband.

"I'm sorry to run out on you," she said, pushing herself up. "This was wonderful, but I've really got to get going. I'm going to be late to the Hamilton farm as it is."

"Of course," he said, waving her concern away. "I've got it. You go."

"It was delicious," Harriet said. She leaned in and kissed him and then ran upstairs to run a comb through her hair and brush her teeth. When she came back downstairs, Will was at the sink, washing dishes. "I love you," she called before dashing out the door.

Harriet had been to the Hamilton farm a few times and found it easily enough. It wasn't too far from the farm where Jim the tortoise lived, in fact. She examined Stella, the roan horse, and administered the first dose of an antibiotic that she promised Doug Hamilton would clear Stella's stomach woes right up.

She drove back to the clinic, and just as she climbed out of the car, her phone rang. Mrs. Lewis. Harriet had met the housekeeper for Beresford Manor several times, and found her to be friendly and helpful, but they didn't usually call each other. She put the phone to her ear. "Hello?"

"Oh, Harriet, I'm so glad I caught you. It's Agatha Lewis. How are you? Are you doing okay? Congratulations on your marriage, by the way. I saw the announcement in the paper. I'm so thrilled for you. The vicar, imagine that. And are you still taking care of animals?"

When she finally paused to take a breath, Harriet didn't even know where to start answering her questions.

"Thank you," she said. "Will is a wonderful man, and we're very happy. And yes, I'm continuing with my practice."

"Oh good. Well, look, I'm calling you because I'm not really sure what to do. Marian says I should talk to the police, but I don't know, it's kind of sensitive, I suppose, and I might be wrong. I don't want to cast aspersions, especially, because, you know. Anyway, you're so good at mysteries, so I thought maybe I would ask you what to do."

Harriet's mind spun from trying to follow her words. "Why don't you tell me what's bothering you?"

"Okay, sure, thank you. Only right now is not great, because I've got to get the baron's breakfast ready, you see, but I was hoping you might be able to talk later? Maybe you could meet me for tea this afternoon?"

"Sure." Harriet was more bewildered by the moment. It seemed like Mrs. Lewis had been in such a rush to speak with her, and now she wanted to wait until this afternoon? But by this point, Harriet was far too curious to turn the invitation down. "What time is good for you?"

"Would four o'clock suit? Maybe at the Happy Cup?"

"That would work fine." The little tearoom in town was charming, and Harriet was always glad for an opportunity to visit.

"All right, I'll see you then. Thank you, Harriet."

Harriet hung up confused, but she told herself she'd find out more later. For now, she had to get to work. She started to walk toward the house, but just as she reached for the door, her phone rang again. Mrs. Lewis again? But no, this time she saw the words AUNT JINNY on the screen.

"Hello?"

"Hello, Harriet. I'm sorry to call so early, but I was hoping to catch you before you began your workday."

"Hi, Aunt Jinny. It's not too early. How are you?"

"I'm doing well. I wanted to let you know I called Peter Robinson, and he's actually working on a book about his great-great-grand-father, which I didn't know. It sounds very interesting. Anyway, he said he's very happy to meet you. He said to pop by any time after eleven and he'll tell you what he can."

"That's wonderful. Thank you so much."

Aunt Jinny gave her the address—though the word *address* implied that the house was on a street, while the fisherman's cottages in the village were all lined up along what basically amounted to narrow alleys.

"It's the blue door next to the yellow one on Martin's Row."

Harriet was pretty sure she could find that. "Thank you so much. I'll go see him on my lunch break."

"Happy to help," Aunt Jinny said.

Harriet ended the call and tucked her phone in her pocket. She wanted to grab a charger, and she needed to let Charlie and Max into the clinic, so she decided to go through the house. It still smelled like bacon and syrup, and she inhaled deeply as she ran to the kitchen to grab the spare charger she kept in the junk drawer. But she came to a screeching halt when she crossed the threshold.

There were dishes piled in the sink, leftover waffles still sitting on a plate, and the crust of a waffle dunked in the dregs of a cup of tea. The waffle iron was covered in batter, as was the granite beneath it. A puddle of sticky syrup pooled on the counter.

Will hadn't cleaned up after his elaborate breakfast. He'd just left a huge mess for her to take care of. She felt anger start to simmer. She hadn't even wanted a big breakfast this morning. She'd intended to grab a quick bite, spend some time reading her Bible, and be out the door early. Sure, it was a nice gesture for him to make the feast, but honestly, it seemed like he'd done it because he wanted waffles and bacon. He hadn't asked her what she wanted, and it was hardly a gift to her if it meant she was left with a trashed kitchen she would be stuck cleaning. He had meetings through this evening. He clearly knew he wouldn't be able to clean it up himself.

Harriet took a deep breath and tried to keep her anger from getting the best of her. Will hadn't meant to make her life more difficult, but how could he be so inconsiderate of her feelings? Surely he knew a pile of dirty dishes left for her would upset her, especially after they'd talked about it two days ago. How did he not get it? Or *did* he get it, and just not care?

Harriet couldn't dwell on that now. She had to get to the clinic. She had a full day ahead of her, and she needed to be focused so she could give her patients the best possible care. She took a few deep breaths, asked the Lord for patience and grace, and then forced a smile onto her face before opening the door between the house and clinic and ushering Max and Charlie and Mercedes through. Ash was nowhere to be seen.

"Hello," Polly said, as Charlie launched himself onto the counter. "How are you?"

"Livid," Harriet admitted. She hadn't intended to tell Polly about it, but seeing her friend there, she couldn't stop herself. "Will cooked a humongous breakfast and didn't clean up after himself. He just left it all for me to clean."

"What did he make?" Polly asked, cocking her head. "Was it good?"

"Waffles and bacon. And yes, it was good, but honestly, he made this big deal about how he did it for me. But I didn't ask for it, and then to leave it to me to clean it all up?" Harriet felt her anger bubbling up again. "How can he be so selfish?"

"Have you talked to him about it?" Polly asked, her voice maddeningly calm. It was the kind of voice a person used when they were trying to talk a child out of a tantrum.

"No, I just got back from the Hamilton farm and saw it. Dishes piled everywhere, syrup and batter on the counter. It's a total mess."

"I can see how that would be frustrating," Polly said, using the same calming tone of voice. "But maybe there's more to the story than you know. Maybe he got an emergency call and someone needed their pastor, stat. Maybe there was a call from the lifeboat brigade, and he rushed to the boat launch."

"Was there? An emergency at sea?"

"I have no idea. I'm just saying, there are all kinds of things that could have made him have to take off. Or maybe he forgot about a meeting or something and had to rush to get there. It happens to the best of us. He probably thought you'd be gone all morning and he'd get back in time to clean it up before you even saw it."

The scenarios Polly suggested weren't totally farfetched, Harriet had to admit. It was possible something like what she suggested had happened. But it was also totally possible Will had been thoughtless.

"Will is crazy about you, Harriet. Everyone can see it. I'm sure he had no intention of frustrating you."

"Yes, but just because he didn't mean to do it doesn't mean it didn't happen," Harriet said.

"Fair enough. And you should talk to him about that. But maybe it's worth assuming the best of him instead of jumping straight to accusing him of being thoughtless and selfish. Because he's neither of those things, most of the time."

Harriet hated that Polly was right. She'd ramped up from zero to sixty in pretty close to an instant. Maybe she'd overreacted. Almost certainly she was still holding on to resentment left over from last night's disagreement. Ugh. She didn't want to admit that maybe she could have been more gracious.

But still, even though she knew all of that, it still felt like Will didn't care. Those dishes felt like him saying that he knew leaving a mess bothered her and it didn't matter to him. She couldn't deny that the hurt she felt—that the message she'd absorbed on seeing them—was real.

"Van and I got into a fight about making the bed the other day," Polly said, smiling guiltily.

"Making the bed?"

"He's pretty good about it, for the most part. Whoever gets up last should make the bed, right? But a lot of times he gets up after me and just leaves it, and it drives me crazy. Last week I got so mad, I threw a pillow at him."

"I suppose there are worse things you could have thrown," Harriet said. "Will's lucky he wasn't around when I saw the waffle iron." She chuckled.

"I shouldn't throw *anything* at my husband," Polly said. "I love him. I promised to love and honor him. But I just got so fed up that I lost my temper."

"Yeah," Harriet said. "Same, probably."

"What I'm trying to say is that I understand," Polly said. "We've made huge changes in our lives. Learning to live with someone is hard no matter how much you love them. But I'd rather get fed up sometimes than not have married him, right?"

"For sure." It wasn't even a question.

"I'm just saying, from one fed-up newlywed to another, maybe give him the benefit of the doubt," Polly said.

She was right. "I'll try," Harriet said. "But he'd better have a good story."

Whatever Polly was about to say in response was cut off when Mrs. Braden walked in, cat carrier balanced on her hip, Jingles howling at the indignity.

"Good morning," Polly said brightly, shifting immediately into cheerful greeting mode. It would take Harriet a moment longer, but she did her best to smile as she ushered Mrs. Braden and Jingles into the exam room.

Over the next few hours, Harriet examined three cats, two dogs, a rabbit, a bearded dragon, and a cockatoo. It was when she was trimming the cockatoo's beak that she had an idea. When they had a break for lunch, she grabbed her microchip scanner and called Mercedes to her. She scooped up the pup and aimed the scanner at her back, at the space between her shoulder blades where the chip would be, if she had one. She pressed the button, and a number came up.

"Polly, could you look up a chip number for me?" Harriet asked.

"Sure. What is it?"

Harriet read out the fifteen-digit number, and Polly looked it up in the registry on her computer.

"Reginald Carruthers, and an address in Dover," she said. "What—is that Mercedes's number?"

"That's what came up when I scanned her chip," Harriet said.

"But she belongs to Annie and Paul." Polly sounded distressed.

"That may well be," Harriet said. She set the dog down, and she scampered off. "But she's registered to Reginald Carruthers."

"How is that possible?" Polly said. "She's in all their videos."

"Maybe they got her from Reginald and he never transferred the registration," Harriet said. "Sometimes people forget to do that. Or—I don't know. There could be any number of reasons, I suppose."

"But they got her from a breeder. She's a purebred. They made a video about it."

"Maybe Reginald is the breeder. Plenty of breeders chip their puppies and then transfer ownership after the puppy is sold."

"And you think he just forgot?"

"I don't know." But she did know that, as the attending veterinarian, she was supposed to contact the owner of record if there were any questions. "Is there a phone number listed?"

"There is," Polly said.

"Let's give it a call." As Polly read out the numbers, Harriet dialed them into her phone.

"Hello?" said a man on the other end of the line.

"I'm looking for a Reginald Carruthers," Harriet said.

"You got 'im. What do you need?"

"My name is Dr. Harriet Bailey-Knight, and I'm a veterinarian in Yorkshire. I'm calling in regards to a Yorkshire terrier whose microchip is registered to you."

"I don't have a dog."

"So you don't know anything about a Yorkshire terrier named Mercedes?"

"I had a dog once. A terrier mix. My daughter got her for me from a shelter. I had her for three years, and then two years ago I had to go into assisted living, and they wouldn't let me keep her. It was really hard to give her up, but I found a nice young couple who could give her a good home."

"I see. Did you ever transfer the information in the microchip records?" Harriet asked.

"I didn't know there was such a thing," Reginald said. "I certainly didn't know she had a chip. If my name came up, my daughter must have done it, and I wouldn't have the slightest clue how to undo it."

He sounded a little upset, so Harriet said, "Don't worry, Mr. Carruthers, we'll take care of getting that changed. Thank you so much for your help."

As soon as Harriet hung up, Polly said, "Is everything they portrayed a lie?"

"I wouldn't go that far," Harriet said. "We don't know what happened here."

"I know they made a video about getting their purebred Yorkie from a breeder, when it turns out they got a mixed breed from a nice old man."

"I suppose it's just one more piece of their story that doesn't add up," Harriet said. There were so many of them at this point. "It doesn't really tell us anything we didn't know though."

"It doesn't change the fact that Mercedes is the sweetest little thing, does it?" Polly scooped the little dog up and buried her face in its fur.

"It doesn't," Harriet said. It was one more piece of the puzzle, but so far, it wasn't adding up to much. Well, she would continue to think on it. "I'm going to run out for a bit."

Polly waved but kept her face buried in Mercedes's fur.

Harriet drove to the parking lot in the upper part of town and began descending the steps along New Street. About halfway down the hill—and what felt like several hundred steps—a pathway branched off, and Harriet followed the long corridor. She turned when another alleyway branched off to the right. The fisherman's cottages that lined the narrow pathway were tiny, attached homes, almost unbelievably adorable in their compact quaintness. The dwellings had been built hundreds of years ago, before modern building codes, and this little warren of tangled pathways lined with cottages was unlike anything Harriet had seen before.

She followed a set of steps and found the house with its bright blue door. She knocked, and a moment later it was opened by a man with gray hair, glasses, and lively blue eyes. He wore corduroys and a thick wool sweater and smiled when he saw her.

"Harriet?"

"Hi, Mr. Robinson."

"Please, you must call me Peter," he said. "You're Doc Bailey's granddaughter?"

"That's right," Harriet said. "You knew him?"

"Everyone knew your grandfather." He stepped back and gestured for her to come inside. "Please, come in."

"Thank you."

She stepped into a room with a low ceiling and a huge fireplace, stuffed with a couch, two big chairs, and a television. There was hardly room to move around, but the crackling fire in the fireplace was warm and inviting. Most of the cottages had been upgraded with modern heating systems, but when they were built, fire would have been the only way to heat the homes.

"Please have a seat." He gestured to the couch. "Can I get you a cup of tea?"

Harriet loved the tradition of offering tea to a guest at any time of the day or night. She'd gotten used to the fact that there was pretty much no situation that didn't call for it, and she'd learned it was best to accept when it was offered. "That would be lovely."

"I'll be right back," Peter said. After he left the room, she sat in one of the chairs and looked around, taking in the faded floral wallpaper, the knitted throw, the paintings of women in Victorian dress on the walls. A woman lived here, she assumed, or at least had at some point.

"Here we are," he said, returning with two cups and saucers. A bag of Earl Grey rested in the cup he handed her. He set his own cup down, left the room again, and returned a moment later with sugar and milk, and then he sat in the other chair.

"So," he said, smiling, "your aunt told me you wanted to know about my great-great-grandfather, Trueman Robinson."

"That's right," Harriet said. "And about the wreck of the *Visiter*."

"There's no subject I'd love to talk about more. Did Jinny tell you I've been writing a book about him?"

"She did." Harriet squeezed out the tea bag with her spoon and set it on the saucer. "It's impressive."

"It's just a project to keep me busy, really," he said. "I retired a few years ago, and after my wife passed last year, I needed a project."

"I'm sorry about your wife."

"Thank you. It's strange to try to make my way without her. We were married for fifty-two years. Can you imagine?"

"That sounds like an accomplishment worth celebrating." She hoped she and Will would live long enough to have fifty-two years together. She thought about the dishes in the sink and pushed the image from her mind as her heart rate started to speed up.

"You're married?" he asked, nodding at her left hand.

"That's right. Just a few weeks now. My husband is the vicar of White Church."

"Ah, Pastor Will. I'd heard he'd gotten married. So you're the lucky woman."

"I am." She added a small scoop of sugar and a splash of milk to her tea and sat back.

"I'm not religious myself," Peter said. "But I've always liked Pastor Will. He seems like a stand-up guy."

"He's pretty great," Harriet admitted. "What's your secret to a long marriage?"

"Have a short memory," he said without a moment of hesitation. "Forgive, move on quickly, and then don't bring it up again."

For a moment, Harriet wondered if he somehow knew about how her evening and morning had gone. Then she realized that was crazy. "That's good advice."

"Tricky to do, I'll admit. Especially in those first years, we disagreed a lot. It's natural, as you're learning to live and build a life together. But stick with it, and have a short memory, and it will all come right in the end."

She had every intention of sticking with it. She'd meant it when she said "till death us do part." But the bit about forgiving and moving on quickly was something to consider.

"Look at me, babbling on," he said. "You didn't come here to hear about an old man's past."

"Actually, that's exactly what I came here for," Harriet said. "Or your family's past, at least."

"All right then. I could go on for hours about Trueman, but I know you have to get back to work, so I'll give you the truncated version. My great-great-grandfather grew up in this house. His family were fishermen for generations before that. The documents are spotty from that long ago, but my best guess is that my ancestors first moved here in the 1710s or so."

"Wow." Harriet knew the cottages were old, but still.

"Trueman was born in 1849 and worked on boats his whole life, as did most everyone around here then."

"Fishing?" Harriet asked.

"Fishing, sure, but most of the money was in shipping. Back then, that was how goods were moved around, especially when you lived on an island with imperialist dreams. Many of the men in these parts signed on to long journeys on ships that took them all the way to the other side of the world, though most of the trading was done with the continent or within England. It was hard work and took men away from their families for months or even years at a time. It was also very dangerous. So many ships were lost at sea, and returning safely home was never a guarantee."

He picked up his cup and took a long sip then set it down and continued.

"My great-great-grandfather was on the crew of several large ships and managed to gain some money and experience. By the time he was thirty, he'd purchased his own ship, the *Visiter*. She was already quite old by that point, but she was seaworthy, and he started captaining his own voyages out of Whitby."

Whitby would have been the closest port that could handle large sailing ships. White Church Bay had the spillway where small craft could be launched, but there was no marina or dock, because the bay was too shallow to allow larger ships to get close.

"He must have been a good businessman in addition to a good sailor," Harriet said.

"Well, he was shrewd, I'll say that."

Harriet cocked her head.

"The evidence suggests that part of what made Trueman so successful was his willingness to, bend the rules, shall we say?"

"Ah." Harriet understood. "I read that the *Visiter* carried a load of coal, but judging by the things that washed up on shore after the wreck, it sounds like there was more than coal on board."

"Exactly," he said. "Of course, he wasn't alone in this. I'm sure you've heard that our little town was known as a smuggler's haven."

"I know there are tunnels under some of the buildings in town and that goods could be brought inland without being seen."

"That's right. Most of them are sealed up now, of course. We use the space for storage these days, but there were several active tunnels a century and a half ago."

"That's amazing."

"All the cottages along this row were connected to the tunnel. Well, anyway, like I said, that space is used for storage now. When I started working on this book, I went down there and brought up all the boxes I could find that held documents from Trueman's time."

"You have documents from back then in your basement?"

"Oh, there are things much earlier than that down there."

"You don't want to donate those things to a library or museum? Or the historical society?"

"I would have to sort it all out before I could do that, now wouldn't I? Maybe that's my next project. But for now, I have all the Trueman files out on my table. Come see." He pushed himself up and started toward the narrow hall. Harriet followed him, the old floorboards creaking beneath their feet, until they came to a snug kitchen with an Aga range, a farmhouse sink with a floral curtain hung under it, and a narrow fridge and freezer. A compact wooden table sat in the corner, and stacks of papers covered every inch of its surface. Some were the dark brownish yellow of old documents, and others were the bright white of printer paper.

"After Jinny called, I started digging around in the ship's manifests, which I knew I'd seen in here somewhere," Peter said.

"You have ship's manifests from a hundred and forty years ago here?" Harriet eyed the stacks of papers. It was incredible and kind of nuts that he would have this stuff sitting in his basement.

"And in the crawl space under the roof, as well. When my ancestors died, their things ended up in storage. Maybe we're a family of packrats, I don't know. I just know that there are all kinds of things around here, and I was able to find these." He pointed to a stack of yellowed papers. "He had two sets of ledgers, of course, but luckily, he kept them both. And here"—he tapped the paper on the top of the stack—"is the list of everything that was brought on board the *Visiter* before it set off from Newcastle. The real list, and then the one for the authorities beneath it. Jinny said you were interested in the tortoise, and that's on there."

Harriet wanted to reach for the papers, but caution stopped her. "Should I use gloves or something?" She didn't want to be responsible for ruining the historical documents.

"Don't be silly. They've survived this long. They'll be fine."

She reached for the paper and squinted at the ornate script. The list had been written with a fine-nibbed pen but with a shaky hand, and the old-fashioned letters made it even harder to read. But she could make it out.

Coal: 5 tonnes
Flour: 2 barrels
Baking powder: 1 jar
Tea: 10 jars
Sugar: 1 cup
Oil, for cooking: 3 jugs
Dried meat: 50 pounds
Cakes of soap: 3

The manifest went on for several pages, listing all the necessities for a long sea voyage. Near the end, she found what she was looking for.

To be unloaded in White Church Bay:
Whiskey: 4 barrels
1 sapphire necklace
1 painted screen from the Orient
1 ivory comb
1 African tortoise, marked with the letters JM
4 barrels sugar
12 jars of spices from India

There it was. The tortoise had the letters *JM* engraved on it. That was Jim. But how did the *I* get there, if he had only *J* and *M* carved into his shell back then? Had someone added the *I* at some point? Or—wait, was the *I* even part of the carving? She remembered it looked more like a marking on the shell. In any case, it didn't really matter. She now had proof that the tortoise that lived on Rupert's farm was indeed the tortoise that was on the *Visiter*, headed for the home of Lord Beresford.

She let the knowledge sink in. The tortoise somehow not only survived the shipwreck and made it to shore but survived the hundred and fortysomething years since. For not the first time, Harriet wished animals could talk. The tales that tortoise could probably tell… She couldn't wrap her mind around how vastly the world had changed in Jim's lifetime. Of course, a tortoise wouldn't understand the importance of the lightbulb, the internal combustion engine, or the internet, but still.

"This is incredible," Harriet said. "This tortoise—it's still alive."

"It's what?"

"It's alive and living on a farm outside Fylingthorpe."

"You're joking."

"I'm not. Tortoises can live a very long time."

"I should say so, if you're telling me this is the same one. My goodness. It beggars belief. How do you know it's the same one?"

"It says here this one had JM carved into its shell. Check this out." Harriet opened the photos app on her phone and scrolled until she found the pictures she'd taken of Jim.

"That's incredible," Peter said. He used two fingers to zoom in. "It's really the same tortoise. How is that possible?"

"It obviously survived the wreck somehow. Tortoises are land animals, and they don't swim, but somehow it got to shore."

"But how did it get from shore to a farm outside Frylingthorpe?" Peter asked.

"I don't know," Harriet admitted. "But that's the next thing I want to find out."

CHAPTER FOURTEEN

Harriet found Mrs. Lewis sitting at a table by the window of the Happy Cup. Harriet waved and slid into the chair across from her. The place was bustling and felt inviting. Their little round table was covered with a floral tablecloth and had a tiny vase with fresh pansies in it.

"Hello, dear," Mrs. Lewis said. "Take off your coat. You look good. Married life is treating you well, is it?"

"It is," Harriet said. "It's nice to see you."

Linda Granville approached the table and set two menus down in front of them. Harriet knew her Labrador, Bailey, and had also treated some of the other animals on Linda's small farm.

"Good afternoon," Linda said, smiling. "Good to see you, Doc. Hello, Agatha." She nodded at each of them in turn. "I'll give you a moment to take a look at the menu."

"No need, on my end," Mrs. Lewis said. "I'll have a pot of Yorkshire Red please, and one of those lovely currant scones."

"Of course," Linda said. "And do you know what you want, Doc?"

"Goodness." Harriet scanned the menu. The Full Afternoon at the next table, with its three-level tray loaded with delicate pastries, fruit tarts, and finger sandwiches, looked divine. But she didn't need all that so close to dinner, sadly. "I'll have a pot of Earl Grey, please."

"Go on, get a scone too. You won't regret it," Mrs. Lewis said.

"All right." Harriet gave in. "I'll take a lemon scone, please."

"Coming right up."

"So," Mrs. Lewis said, as soon as Linda was out of earshot, "thank you for meeting with me. I figured this place is always buzzing enough that people won't be able to overhear our conversation."

"Of course." Harriet could think of plenty of places where they wouldn't be overheard, including her own office, but Mrs. Lewis seemed quite happy to be here. "So what was it you wanted to talk to me about?"

"Like I said on the phone, it's a bit sensitive. It has to do with those missing sailors. You've heard about them?"

"Indeed, I have," Harriet said. Boy, had she. But she didn't want to go into how involved she was.

"I saw it in the paper yesterday, and I couldn't believe it. How could a couple go missing off their boat, just like that? Just vanished? It doesn't make any sense."

"It is perplexing," Harriet said.

"I called Marian straightaway." Harriet had met Mrs. Lewis's daughter. "I said, how could something like that happen? How could two people go missing off a boat like that, with the boat just left floating on the water? It's madness. Marian thought it was very strange too, and she suggested they'd met up with someone bad, you know what I mean? Someone like one of those pirates you read about? Someone who might have… Well, anyway, people think pirates are all in the past, and that they're this funny thing, like 'yo-ho-ho and a bottle of rum' and dressing up like Blackbeard and with a pegleg and whatnot for costume parties, but it's really quite evil what they do, isn't it? Taking people captive, stealing treasure off people's boats? It's horrible, isn't it?"

It sounded to Harriet like Mrs. Lewis's image of pirates had been shaped by popular culture as much as anyone else's, but she let her continue.

"And they're all over the seas these days. Colin—that's Marian's husband, you see, he's a fisherman, like, for his job—Colin says that pirates aren't so much a threat around these parts, but there are other parts of the world that are more dangerous, you see, but I don't know. It seems like bad things happen all over the world these days, don't they?"

"So you think pirates may have kidnapped the sailors?" Harriet didn't see why they'd needed to come here if that was her news.

"Oh no, that was just what Marian said at first, when she and I spoke about it after we read the paper. We also had lots of other ideas. Of course, the newspaper made it sound like they may have been washed overboard, and I hope that's not true. But it also made it sound like the police weren't sure that was it, didn't it?"

"What kinds of ideas did you and your daughter have?" Harriet asked.

"I thought they might have tied up at the marina but might not have tied up very well, you see? And then they'd gone into town and the boat slipped away from the dock and floated out to sea. And then they were so embarrassed they slipped away and didn't want to come forward and claim the boat, not once it was such big news. Marian says that's not possible, at least not without a lot of people noticing, but I don't know. You wouldn't necessarily notice a boat leaving the harbor, would you?"

The docks for the pleasure boats were fairly deep in the harbor. This possibility seemed exceedingly unlikely to Harriet, but she didn't say that. Plus, the sails had been unfurled, and they wouldn't have been open if the boat had been tied up at the dock.

"Marian said that was crazy, that even if the sailboat had somehow been dragged out to sea, they would have claimed it straightaway, because the boat was worth over a hundred thousand pounds. A hundred thousand pounds! Can you imagine? You could buy a home for that in some parts of the county. Who would spend that much on a boat?"

She was interrupted by Linda returning, carrying a tray with two teapots wrapped in quilted cozies and two plates with scones on them, among other things. "Here you are," she said, placing a pot of tea in front of each of them. She added a small pitcher of milk and a bowl of sugar cubes. She set down the plates of scones, each with a bowl of clotted cream and another of jam, and two saucers with a silver tea strainer on top of each. "Do you need anything else?"

"No, thank you," Harriet said. Linda smiled and left to wait on another table.

"Lovely." Mrs. Lewis turned over the teacup that sat at her place setting, set the tea strainer on top, and poured out her tea. Harriet did the same, and the earthy scent of Earl Grey rose from the cup.

"So, anyway, after Marian pooh-poohed my idea, I said, well, what do *you* think happened then? Marian suggested they vanished on purpose. I said that was silly, why would they do that, and Marian said maybe because they owed a lot of money to someone. But really, if you can afford a boat like that, how could you be in debt? Marian also suggested that maybe they'd broken the law and wanted everyone to think they were dead so they could slip away and escape to some other country, or that the whole thing was one big publicity stunt, or that it was some sort of hazing ritual gone wrong, which doesn't even make sense. They weren't in college, pledging a fraternity or sorority, now were they?"

Harriet added a sugar cube and a splash of milk to her cup and used a tiny silver spoon to stir.

"She also suggested maybe one of them was swimming off the side of the boat and got into trouble and the other jumped in to save them and they both drowned. But I said, have you felt the North Sea in September? It's freezing. Why would anyone go for a dip? But Marian said that was why they would have drowned, because the water is so cold your body starts shutting down right away."

Harriet began to wonder whether there was actually something Mrs. Lewis had brought her here to ask, or whether she just wanted someone to bounce ideas off of. She set the spoon aside and took a sip of the tea, which was very good. She broke off a piece of the scone and ate it. It was delicious. If nothing else came out of this meeting, at least she'd gotten some nice refreshments out of it.

"So anyway, I had to go to work. You know the baron is very particular about how his house is run, so I put it out of my mind and tried to focus. I had a job to do, you know. And I did it, until that evening, when Marian called me again, all in a tizzy. I thought something had happened to Grant, she was so worked up"—Grant was her young grandson—"but then she told me that when Colin came home from work, she asked him about the missing boaters, and he said he'd heard all about it, because the Coastguard asked all the boats in the area to be on the lookout for the missing sailors, so he'd been looking for them all week. And he hadn't even mentioned it to Marian, can you believe it? She was upset, let me tell you, because she apparently loves their videos. Did you know they make videos and put them online, and that's their job? Who ever heard of such a thing? Well, anyway, Colin said that he'd heard all sorts of theories about what happened to them and didn't know what was really true, but he told her he'd seen something odd at the marina and thought maybe he should let the police know."

Finally, they were getting somewhere.

"What did Colin see?" Harriet asked, taking another sip of tea.

"Well, apparently Colin's boat went out early on Sunday morning, because of the tides, you see. The high tide was at four a.m., so they went out around two, because his boat is so large it can only go through the harbor when the tide is at least most of the way in."

"He went out fishing at two in the morning on Sunday?"

"They fish at all times. Depends on the tides, like I said."

"Okay, but isn't there a high tide again twelve hours later? Why didn't they go out Sunday afternoon instead?"

"That's when the Sheffield United game would be on, wouldn't it? They're not going to go fishing when the game is on, are they?"

Harriet nodded, as if this made perfect sense. She knew how dedicated to their soccer teams the people around here were. They were like football fans back home, only more so.

"I suppose not." Harriet took another sip of tea. "So, what did Colin see?"

"Says he saw Shane O'Grady taking his boat out at the same time."

The way Mrs. Lewis said it, Harriet could tell she was supposed to be shocked, but she played the words back through her head and didn't see what was so surprising about them.

"Maybe he was going out fishing, as well?" she ventured.

"At *that* time?"

Harriet felt like she was losing her mind. "You just said that was when Colin took his boat out fishing."

"Yes, because Colin's boat is huge. It's a right trawler. You can't get that thing out at low tide. You'd get stuck right in the middle of the harbor. But Shane's boat is a cabin cruiser. A big one, made for fishing, but ever since all that stuff with the shellfish, he doesn't have a proper commercial boat anymore, does he? His hull is small enough it could go out at pretty much any time."

Shane O'Grady's commercial license had been withdrawn after a series of incidents that proved him to be less than honest, including unplugging a competitor's refrigerated fish tank and stealing mussels. He still fished regularly, but he didn't seem to have gone back to a commercial trade.

"I saw him down at the marina on Sunday," Harriet said. "His boat is big but definitely not the size of a commercial boat."

"Right. So why would he be going out in his boat from the marina in the middle of the night?"

"Maybe he wanted to watch the football game on Sunday afternoon?" Harriet ventured.

"He could have gone out in the morning and still made it back on time for the game," Mrs. Lewis said. "Besides, he's a Manchester fan."

"So he wouldn't be watching a game Sunday afternoon?" Didn't they all play on Sundays?

"Well, of course he could be, but you can't trust a Manchester fan, now can you?"

Harriet's head spun. She didn't see what one thing had to do with another.

"So you're saying it's suspicious that he took his boat out in the middle of the night." Harriet was pretty sure that was what her friend was getting at, even if she didn't understand that logic.

"That's right." Mrs. Lewis slathered her scone with jam and clotted cream.

"But it wasn't suspicious for Colin to be doing the same thing."

"Right."

"Because of the size of the boat?"

"Because of the size of the boat, and because, well, because it was Shady O'Grady." Mrs. Lewis popped a bite of the scone into her mouth.

"I see." Harriet had heard it said that if something strange was going on at the marina, Shane O'Grady was probably behind it. But he'd changed his ways. At least, that was what he told her back in the spring, and by all accounts, it seemed to be true. There'd been no rumors of anything shady in months, and he'd sponsored a youth soccer team over the summer. He had even come to church a few times. "But he's on the straight and narrow, from what I understand."

"That's why I wanted to talk to you about it," Mrs. Lewis said. "Because I know he's been keeping his nose clean. Says he doesn't do that stuff anymore. So, like I said on the phone, I don't want to cast aspersions. If he's got nothing to do with it, I'd hate to be the one to get him interrogated by the police."

"But obviously you think something doesn't add up."

"I would also hate to not report it, if it does mean something," Mrs. Lewis said. "I mean, what if he was involved and I was too worried about hurting his feelings to say anything and he got off scot-free? That would be terrible."

"It sounds like you have a decision to make," Harriet said.

"That's why I wanted to talk to you. I thought maybe you could... well, you know. You're investigating this mystery, aren't you?"

"Not in any official way," Harriet said. "The police and the Coastguard are involved, and I'm trying to stay out of the way."

"But you're also looking into it yourself, aren't you? After all, the police investigated when the baron went missing, but you were the one who found him. And you were the one who looked into that missing statue from the baron's collection. I thought surely you'd be all over this."

"So you want me to find out if it was Shane O'Grady being shady again or whether he was just going about his business?"

"I was thinking so, yes. Because then, he's not in trouble with the police if there was nothing shady in it, right? But if he was doing something shady after all, then you could tell the police, and they could catch him."

"I see." Harriet spread a section of her scone with jam and clotted cream and took a bite. It really was delicious.

"So? You will?"

Harriet didn't want to say yes. But she also didn't know how to say no, not when it was true she was looking into the mystery in her own way.

"I'll see if I can talk to him," she said.

Mrs. Lewis smiled.

CHAPTER FIFTEEN

Harriet mulled over the conversation with Mrs. Lewis as she walked back up the hill, trying to decide what to do with what the housekeeper had told her. As she walked, she thought about what it meant if Colin truly had seen Shane going out of the marina at two o'clock on Sunday morning.

If it was true, it could indeed be indicative of something improper going on. But it could also be completely innocent. Harriet still didn't totally understand or buy the logic that it was normal for Colin's fishing boat to go out at odd hours of the night, but not Shane O'Grady's. And it was true that Shane certainly did have a reputation for not always following the rules. There was a reason his nickname was *Shady* O'Grady. But also, she thought he was sincere about trying to be better. People could change.

As she walked, she thought about something else. She'd seen him at the dock on Sunday. He'd been working on his boat. Something about a hose of some kind. What had he said? She tried to remember, but whatever it was, it was gone. Some boat-related thing that meant nothing to her. What she did remember, was that whatever it was, Shane said it broke on Saturday and he'd been working on it all day, and Kyle said that he wouldn't have been able to go anywhere until he got it fixed. Which would have made it impossible for him to have taken his boat out on Sunday morning.

Which meant that either Shane was lying about his boat, or Colin was wrong about seeing the boat heading out. Had Colin been confused? There were plenty of boats in the marina, and many of them had that second-story driving-area thing. Maybe he saw a different boat and thought it was Shane's. The second option seemed far more plausible than the first. Why would Shane lie about having a problem with his boat's motor if there was nothing wrong? He was a fisherman. If he didn't go out and fish, there was nothing to sell. He wouldn't have hung out at the dock all day, pretending to fix a hose problem that didn't exist. It was far more likely Colin was confused.

But there was one way maybe she could find out.

By the time Harriet made it back to the parking lot at the top of the hill, she was out of breath and had made up her mind to head over to the marina. They had to have cameras there. Every place had security cameras these days. And hadn't that message board said there were cameras there? The footage would show whether Shane's boat truly had gone out after he'd said his fuel line was broken. She'd stop in at the harbor master's office and see if they'd share the security camera footage with her. If they did, she'd take a look at it. And if they didn't, at least her asking about it might tip them off that there could be something worth investigating on it.

Harriet drove over the gently rolling hills, past low stone walls, fields of purple heather and bright yellow rapeseed, and dozens of woolly sheep. The ruins of Whitby Abbey appeared on the horizon, the golden stone a striking contrast to the bright blue sky, and then as she crested a hill, the town came into view, buildings rising up on either side of the Esk River. She made her way to the marina, parked in the familiar lot, and started toward the harbor master's office.

It was closed. She could see that as she drew close. The lights were off, and the door was shut. She tried the knob, just in case, but it didn't turn. She checked her watch. They must have closed at five. She was a few minutes too late.

Well, that was a wasted trip. She turned around and started for the car again, and as she did, she scanned the docks. There was the sailboat, tied up securely at the Coastguard dock. It was on the far side of the marina, so she would have to walk around the full length to get to it. Should she try? It might be worth it, if she could get on board again and check it out. But it seemed unlikely they would let her, if it was a potential crime scene. Besides, she didn't see anyone there and seriously doubted she'd be able to talk her way onto the Coastguard dock anyway.

She scanned the marina, looking for Kyle's boat. It was there, in its berth, and...

Was that Shane? She stepped forward and squinted, and sure enough, it looked like Shane O'Grady on the dock. She watched him for a moment, trying to decide whether to go talk to him, and then she decided she might as well. She'd come all this way. What could it hurt to talk to him, maybe see what he had to say?

Harriet started to make her way to the dock but then remembered that there was a locked gate blocking her way and only people who moored boats there had the key. It meant that unauthorized people couldn't get access. And she was unauthorized.

She was standing at the gate, debating whether she should call to Shane, when she saw a man on the other side walking toward her.

She couldn't see what boat he'd stepped off of, but in any case, she plastered a big smile on her face and tried to look like she belonged there. When he reached the gate, the man opened it and stepped through then held it open for her.

"Thank you," she said, walking past him. She heard the gate clang shut behind her and walked out to where Shane's boat was tied up. She approached just as he hoisted a trash bag off the bench and was about to step out of the boat.

"Oh." He quickly added, "Sorry. I didn't expect to see you there."

"That's all right," Harriet said. "Sorry to startle you."

"It's okay. It's—" He craned his neck, looking down the dock. "How did you get in here?"

"The guy who just left let me in," she said, gesturing behind her. The man was gone, whoever he was.

"Not supposed to do that," he said. He stood on the deck of the boat, which sat a few feet below the dock. From where she stood she could see a closed door that led to the covered space in the bow of the boat. He set the plastic bag back on the bench. "Must have been Ricky. How did he know you're not here to vandalize the boats?"

"I promise I'm not here to vandalize the boats," Harriet said wryly.

"*I* know that," he said. "'Minister's Wife Gone Rogue.' That would be quite the headline. I know you're not going to steal anything, but *he* didn't know that. I'll talk to Ricky later."

"That sounds very sensible," she said. "Hey, I'm glad I caught you. I actually wanted to ask you about something."

"Yeah?"

What did she want to ask? In the awkwardness that yawned as she tried to think of something, she heard the screech of gulls and the roar of a boat's motor in the distance. Finally, she realized the silence had stretched out too long, and she had to say something. "How's your boat?"

"How's my boat?" He looked at her like she was crazy. "Good? I guess?"

"I'm asking because when I saw you on Sunday, you said something about your motor being busted. A fuel line or something?"

"That's right," he said. "The fuel hose. The marine store didn't have the right part in stock. They say it'll be in tomorrow. How can it take that long? Cost me a week of fishing."

"I'm sorry to hear that," Harriet said. "I know boats can be very expensive to repair when they break. At least that's what Will says when I ask why he doesn't have one."

"Indeed. And like I said, I'm out a week's work, to boot. Maybe I should find a different line of work. Maybe I could be a lawyer or something. They seem to do fine around here. At least, all of mine have." He laughed. "Well, if that's all—"

"You know what's strange?" Harriet said quickly. She would have to be bold. "Someone told me they saw your boat leaving the marina on Saturday night. Or more like Sunday morning, really early. But they couldn't have, right? Your boat was here with a fuel line problem, wasn't it?"

He narrowed his eyes. "Who told you that?"

"It was some fishermen who thought they saw you." Harriet did her best to dodge the question.

"It definitely wasn't me," Shane said. "Like I told you before, my boat's been out of commission since Saturday."

"I guess they must have been confused," Harriet said.

"Guess so. There's a lot of boats around here that look like mine," Shane said, gesturing around. Sure enough, that raised driving tower seemed to be a popular feature. She'd never really noticed it before, but there were a least a dozen or so boats with a similar design in that area of the marina. "It was probably one of them."

"I'm sure it was," Harriet said.

"Well, thanks for checking in." Shane picked up the trash bag again. "It was good to see you."

"Good to see you too," Harriet said. Through the thin plastic of the bag, she could see a bunch of takeaway bags and cartons, some with the logo of a local fish and chips shop. Her stomach started growling, just thinking of fish and chips. They'd had Cliffside Chippy Tuesday night. Was it too soon to have that again?

"Tell Pastor Will I said hi." He stepped up on the bench and then onto the gunnel and over onto the dock. "Please let him know I liked his sermon last week. The one about Jesus telling the fishermen where to throw their nets." He grinned. "Any sermon about getting more fish is okay by me."

"I'll be sure to tell him," Harriet said. Will had preached about the passage a week and a half ago. In the story from Luke, Jesus told Peter and James and John—lifelong fishermen—where to cast their nets. They'd resisted, believing there were no fish around, but relented and were surprised when they hauled up nets overflowing with fish. The point of Will's sermon was that one could trust the words of Jesus, and she could see how Shane would have liked the part about getting lots of fish.

He stood next to her on the dock, waiting for her to start walking to the gate, then followed a step or two behind her.

"Have a good night," she said, waving as she held the gate open for him.

"You too," he said. He let the gate close behind him, and she thought about their conversation all the way to the car.

The phone that had turned on and hit a cell tower in Whitby—was there any chance Shane had the phone?

But he wasn't Shady O'Grady anymore. He'd changed. Hadn't he? She didn't know what to think.

As she walked back to her car, she wondered if she should call Van and tell him what Colin thought he'd seen.

She wanted to take Shane at his word.

Still, as she buckled herself in and turned on the car, Harriet made a decision.

She pulled out her phone.

CHAPTER SIXTEEN

Harriet got ahold of Van and told him what Mrs. Lewis had told her and what Shane O'Grady had said about his boat being out of commission starting on Saturday.

"One of them isn't telling the truth," Van said.

"Or Colin could be mistaken," Harriet said. "We don't know for sure. But I thought—well, anyway, Shane said it definitely wasn't him, and I want to believe him, but I thought it was worth checking. I went to the harbor master's office to see if they would let me see the security camera footage. I figured there had to be cameras set up around the marina. But the office was closed."

"Just as well. There are cameras, but they probably wouldn't have showed it to you anyway," Van said. "But I'll try first thing in the morning."

"You'll let me know what you find?"

"I'll let you know what I can," he said.

Harriet ended the call. On the drive home she thought about the conversations she'd had that day and what she'd learned, and then she thought about Will and what she was going to make for dinner, and about—

She felt her pulse speed up as she thought about those dishes left in the sink. She couldn't believe that, after everything she'd dealt with today, she was going to have to wash the dishes and clean the kitchen too. The syrup was probably congealed into glue by now, and the waffle iron was a lost cause. They'd never get all the caked-on batter off that thing.

She parked in the driveway and was surprised to see Will's car there. He was supposed to have a meeting until six. She'd thought she'd have some time to prepare before she had to talk to him about the dishes. She walked up the path, took a deep breath, and opened the door. Maxwell ran to greet her, and she was hit with the smell of browning onions and cooking meat.

"Hello," Will called from the kitchen.

"I didn't expect you to be home yet," she called back.

"Cecil Weathersby got sick, so we canceled the deacon's meeting. Isn't that great?"

"I don't know that I would call one of your parishioners getting sick great," Harriet said. "But I'm glad to see you."

And she was. Even though she'd been simmering with resentment all day, her heart still warmed when she heard his voice. She hung up her coat and set her bag by the door, and then she walked down the hall to the kitchen and—

It was spotless. The counters were scrubbed clean, the sink was empty, the syrup was wiped up, and the dishwasher was running, filling the room with its low hum. Will stood at the stove, stirring something in a saucepan.

"You cleaned the kitchen."

"Oh dear. I was hoping you hadn't seen it." He shook his head. "I'm so sorry, Harriet. I hope that didn't stress you out too much. I fully intended to clean everything up before I left for my ten o'clock meeting, but then Imogene McAllister called to say that her mother wasn't likely to make it through the day and that Gladys was asking for me."

"Oh." She felt her stomach clench. Polly had been right. The reality of what had happened this morning hit her, and she felt a stab of guilt. "You left the dishes in the sink because you went to sit with a parishioner as she was dying."

Will set the wooden spoon down and nodded.

And suddenly she realized how horrible she'd been, simmering with anger all day that he hadn't wiped up some syrup, when he'd been called to do something eternally important.

"I'm sorry, Harriet, I know how you don't like—"

"Will, it's okay." She stepped forward and took his hands. "Is she…?"

"She died peacefully in her sleep just after noon," he said. "With her children and grandchildren around her. We sang hymns as she passed. I like to think that 'Blessed Assurance' was the last thing she heard as she was ushered into the arms of God."

Harriet bit her lip, fighting tears, but quickly lost that battle. "I'm so sorry, Will."

He rubbed his thumb across the back of her hand.

"What an awful day," she said.

But Will shook his head. "Attending the passing of a member of my congregation isn't my favorite way to spend a day," he said. "But I know what an honor it is. What a privilege to be present during someone's final moments."

She put her arms around him and pulled him into a hug. "I'm so glad you could be there."

"I'm glad I could too," Will said. "But I'm sorry it meant I left this place such a wreck. I never intended to do that to you."

"You obviously had more important things to deal with." While she'd been running around learning about a tortoise, he'd witnessed someone cross into eternity. Everything she'd done that day, and everything that seemed like such a big deal, suddenly paled in comparison.

"Nothing is more important than you," he said. "I will never do something on purpose that would upset you. I promise you that. And I know that leaving the kitchen the way I did probably made you angry."

"It was just some syrup," she said, leaning her head against his chest. She could feel the steady beat of his heart. The truth was it had always been just some syrup. Even if he'd left the mess on purpose, it wasn't something that couldn't be cleaned up. She needed to give him more grace. She needed to not jump to conclusions. She shouldn't assume he was being selfish and self-absorbed when in fact he was the most unselfish man she'd ever met. They stayed like that, in each other's arms, for she didn't know how long. But she finally pulled away and sniffed.

"I think something is burning," she said gesturing at the stove.

"Oh dear," Will said, just as the smoke alarm went off. He dashed to turn the flame off, but by that time, it was too late. The chicken was blackened, and gray smoke wafted up to the ceiling. She raced to the window and threw it open, and Will waved a towel underneath the smoke alarm.

"Well, it was going to be chicken and rice," he said, once they got the alarm shut off.

"It sounds like it would have been lovely," she said, laughing.

"How does fish and chips sound instead?"

She might just get what she'd wanted all along anyway. She smiled up at her kind, gentle, godly husband waving a tea towel and wearing her frilly apron. "That sounds perfect."

CHAPTER SEVENTEEN

After dinner and after the take-out containers were thrown away and the pans scrubbed, Will said he needed to get some work done on his sermon for Sunday. He headed to the study with his laptop, hoping to make up for the time he'd missed while sitting with the McAllisters.

There was plenty of work Harriet could do too—catching up on billing and invoicing, laundry, writing thank-you notes for the wedding gifts they'd received. But she was jumbly, and all she could think about was those missing boaters and Shane O'Grady and Anthony Maglione and Annie and Paul and Jim the tortoise, and all she really wanted to do was try to see if she could figure out what she was missing. There were so many clues, so many theories, so many rumors and gut feelings, but nothing solid. It felt like she had a handful of puzzle pieces but couldn't figure out how to put them together in a way that made sense.

The first thing she did was retrieve her laptop and pull up a website where veterinarians discussed peculiar cases they'd encountered. She didn't think much would turn up, but she entered the phrase "can tortoises swim?" and hit return. To her surprise, there were several posts on the topic, and the answer was pretty unequivocal. No, tortoises were big, lumbering land animals. They could not swim. Just as she'd thought.

However, they could—according to at least one vet—float. A Dr. Matt in Youngstown, Ohio, reported seeing a giant tortoise floating along the surface of the water feature in its enclosure at a zoo. Apparently, air had become trapped in its shell and allowed it to bob along the surface, and the tortoise was able to use its legs to essentially dog-paddle to shore. Dr. Matt speculated that this ability to float was what brought the giant tortoise to the Seychelles Islands to begin with—how else would a land-based species have found its way to not just one but several of the islands in the archipelago?

That was an interesting thought. Had Jim floated to shore after the *Visiter* sank?

Harriet didn't think she could learn anything more definite than that, so she returned to the idea she'd had earlier when she was researching Anthony Maglione, and looked up the driving distance between White Church Bay and Hull. It would take nearly two hours. She checked her work calendar for the next day and saw that her last appointment was at two. She had an early start to the day, but she'd be done in plenty of time to get to Hull if she wanted to. She was sure the police were talking to Anthony Maglione. He'd shown up at the marina, demanding his boat be released, after all. He was definitely on their radar. But if he did have anything to do with Annie and Paul's disappearance, it might not be the best idea to go to talk to him herself. Still, she was tempted. He'd met Annie and Paul. He knew the boat. He would be able to tell her things she didn't know.

For now, she went back to the message board where she'd seen the messages about Whitby, searching for anything new. Any messages that might be relevant that she'd overlooked. Some kind of explanation about what happened to the Bellinghams. She didn't see anything, so she reread the message she'd seen before, from Neptune: *I have a unique errand I'm looking for help with. I will make it worth your while. Any interest, message me privately to learn more.* Then, just the three replies: the soccer fan making fun of it, the Sharkskin person asking how much, and Nessie saying they were sending a private message. Did this have anything to do with the *Salacia* at all?

She clicked on the screen name SharkSkin and was again taken to the page that showed her all the entries they'd made or commented on. They'd expressed opinions multiple times about the stupidity of other people and the decisions they made, and offered a few helpful tips to messages asking for information about how to navigate the harbor at Whitby. The profile picture was a shark, and one of their comments mentioned they lived in Whitby. That was it.

Then she clicked on Nessie's profile. It was similarly vague—not even a placeholder photo, just a generic *N*—and said their location was Whitby. She read back over the messages they had commented on and, once again, it seemed clear that Nessie had no problem with bending the rules, which made them an intriguing figure in this investigation. But as much as she poked around, she couldn't find anything to suggest who Nessie really was. Maybe someone Scottish.

Looking at these message boards wasn't getting her anywhere. She closed the site and decided she would watch more of Annie and Paul's videos. Maybe there was something in one she hadn't seen yet that would reveal a clue she'd missed. She had no inkling what that might be, but she was out of fresh ideas.

She found their page and scrolled down. The last video she'd seen was from the Isle of Man. The next video in the series started with another ad and then showed them stopping in a town called Androssan. "We made it to Scotland!" Annie declared in the video. Harriet looked up a map and saw that this town was on the west coast, just north of the border, and from the video it didn't look all that different from the towns they'd seen in England so far. Following that were several other stops along the west coast of Scotland, including Port Ellen on the isle of Islay, Oban, Tobermorey, Lochmaddy in the Outer Hebrides, and Kinlochbervie. It seemed at some point, whoever named these towns must have given up trying to come up with real words and just started throwing random letters together.

But what she also noticed was that in between the videos about the stops they made along the way, there were more DISASTER! videos.

The first was *DISASTER! ALMOST BLEW UP OUR BOAT!* In this one, Annie and Paul explained how they forgot to run the bilge blower after docking for the night. Harriet looked it up and found out that a bilge blower is a fan that blows flammable fumes away from the engine compartment. "If you don't want to die in a fiery explosion, it's a good idea, if your engine's been off for a while, to run the bilge blower when you start it again. This time we totally forgot," Paul said. "Luckily, we remembered before we got too far out to sea, and managed to not destroy our boat. Crisis averted this time."

Following that were *DISASTER! NEARLY RAN AGROUND! DISASTER! NEARLY CAPSIZED!* And *DISASTER! ALMOST MISSED OUR PORT!*

In each of the videos, a very excited Annie and Paul recounted what silly thing they'd done to nearly ruin their boat or kill themselves. Harriet knew sailing was dangerous, but apparently, she hadn't had any clear idea of how fraught it could be. Then again, they did seem to encounter a large number of disasters. Was that normal? Or were they just particularly bad at sailing? But people seemed to really like it when terrible things almost happened to them. They got tons of comments and views on those videos—more than on the travelogues. Like, significantly more, actually. That was interesting. And it would explain why they made so many of them. But Harriet didn't have a lot of patience for them. She enjoyed getting a look at a place she'd never been before and didn't have much interest in the silly videos about careless mistakes they made. But it seemed she was in the minority.

She read through some of the comments on one of their more recent videos. Mixed in with notes of love and appreciation, there were several detractors.

You're nothing but lying fakes, wrote BobUnderstood3.

Nothing but a couple of thieves, from AnthonyMag.

Harriet stopped scrolling. She'd read a comment from AnthonyMag before, and now that she saw it, it was incredibly obvious who it was. Anthony Maglione. Commenting directly on their videos.

She *had* to go talk to him.

She watched a video about a couple places in the Orkney Islands the couple visited. They featured puffins, which Harriet wasn't mad about. Puffins were such funny-looking birds, delightfully so. The Shetland Islands, where Will's family was from, was farther north, but Annie and Paul didn't stop there. They did round the northern tip of Scotland and celebrated as they began their journey down the east coast. There was a stop in Wick, and then a long, treacherous voyage to Iverness. Of course there were several disaster videos mixed in as well—*DISASTER! GOT KNOCKED OVER BY THE BOOM!*

DISASTER! FORGOT TO CLOSE THE HATCH AND GOT SOAKED! DISASTER! HALYARD FELL OVER AND GOT TANGLED UP IN THE PROPELLER!

Harriet watched them explore the town of Iverness and was so totally wrapped up in their footage of the soaring cathedral that she didn't hear Will come into the room.

"What are you watching?"

She jumped. "Goodness. You scared me."

"Hey. That's Iverness." He pointed at the screen. "You're watching a video about Scotland?" he asked in his thick brogue.

"I'm watching Annie and Paul. I've hit the Scotland phase of their journey."

"The best phase, you mean."

"It does look like a beautiful country, I have to admit."

"It's more than beautiful. It's stunning. It's like no place else on earth. It's no wonder the English kept trying to claim it as their own for so many centuries."

Harriet smiled. "I'd like to see it someday."

"I'll take you there. We should go soon. It's crazy that you've never seen the place where I was born."

"You've never been to Connecticut," Harriet pointed out.

"I've been to New York City. How different could rural Connecticut be?"

Harriet laughed. "Pretty different."

"Yeah, probably."

"Well, I'd love to see Muckle Roe."

"I'll find a way to make it happen before too long."

She closed the current tab, and the page where she found the driving distance to Hull showed on the screen. Will squinted at it.

"You headed to Hull?" he asked.

"I was thinking about it," she said.

"What's in Hull?"

"Anthony Maglione. He's the one who sold Annie and Paul their sailboat. Eli told us about him. They never paid for the boat, and now he wants it back."

"That's right." And then, "A check that didn't clear." His brow furrowed. "You were thinking of going to talk to this guy?"

"I was."

Will didn't say anything for a moment, but judging from the look on his face, he didn't like the idea.

"What do you know about this guy?" he finally asked.

"He's a cardiologist and has been practicing in Hull for twenty years. He has two grown kids. He likes to sail, garden, and play the cello. He opened his home for the holiday house tour last year."

"He sounds extremely dangerous."

Harriet laughed and rolled her eyes.

"He came to the marina in Whitby and demanded his boat back, right?" Will asked.

"Yes," Harriet admitted. That wasn't a point in his favor.

"When were you thinking of going?"

"My last appointment is at two tomorrow. I was thinking of going after that."

Will was silent. He wasn't telling her she was crazy or asking her not to do something so clearly foolish.

Finally, he said, "If I move a couple of meetings around, I can come with you."

"You can?" She tried not to sound as shocked as she felt that he would even consider it.

"You can't go there on your own, obviously," he said. "This cello-playing cardiologist sounds nice enough, but who knows what the truth is. But if you're determined to go anyway—"

"I said I was thinking about it."

"We both know that means you've already decided and just haven't figured out how to tell me," he said.

He was right. That was exactly what it meant. She just hadn't realized it yet.

"I'm not about to let my wife go off alone on some errand that might prove dangerous," he said. "I promised for better or for worse. So if you're going to do this, it seems like I should be right there beside you."

Harriet couldn't help the grin that spread across her face. "I've never loved you more."

CHAPTER EIGHTEEN

Harriet was administering antibiotics to a flock of sheep before the sun came up the next morning. She'd never get over what funny creatures sheep were, the way they bleated loudly, seemingly randomly. They were cute and woolly and fluffy. They weren't hard to gather up, and she squirted medicine into their mouths, one at a time, until she'd worked her way through the whole flock. Soon she was on her way back to the clinic and got there just as Van dropped Polly off.

"Hey," Harriet said, walking toward the door. Polly hopped out of Van's car, and he waved before turning around and driving out of the lot.

"How were the sheep?" Polly asked as Harriet unlocked the door.

"Loud," Harriet said. "And stinky."

"Sounds like sheep," Polly said, following behind her. "Fortunately, we're done early today, assuming nothing goes wrong."

"Let's hope nothing does." An emergency surgery or other unexpected visit would put a kink in her plans to visit Hull.

"Did you see the page Annie and Paul's fans have put up about them?" Polly asked, settling in at the computer.

"No, I haven't," Harriet said.

"It's just a fan site, nothing official or anything, but people are posting messages and well-wishes and things. There's got to be at least a thousand messages on it. Their fans are really worried."

Polly navigated to the site and showed her. It was a simple message board-style page, where people could post comments. Polly was right, there were a lot of messages, mostly things like *Please be ok, we're thinking about you* and *We love you, Annie and Paul!*

"It's not good that they haven't found them yet, is it?" Polly asked.

"It's hard to say," Harriet said. But then, a second later, she added, "I mean, obviously it's not good that they haven't been found yet. The Coastguard called off the search for them several days ago. If they really were lost on a life raft somewhere, there's not much hope at this point, I'm afraid. But since the police aren't convinced that's what happened, I don't know."

"You think they're out there somewhere?"

"I hope so."

The day started off with a visit from a man named Bernard Donner with a pet lizard that "wasn't acting like himself." Harriet didn't know how to gauge what a lizard should act like, but trusted that its owner knew. She suggested Bernard change the lizard's diet and clean his cage and see if those things helped. She was just finishing giving a newly adopted kitten a checkup—everything looked good—when her cell phone rang. It was Rupert Baker.

She stepped into the hallway to answer it. "Hello?"

"Hi, Harriet. Rupert here."

"Hi, Rupert. How are you?"

"I'm doing all right. Look, I've been thinking about Jim ever since you asked me whether he could have come off the ship that wrecked. I was curious about whether it was possible. At first, I'll admit, I didn't believe you when you said tortoises could be that old. I know Jim has been around at least since my grandfather's time, but we thought he was really pushing it, on his last legs. I told my wife you were nuts, truth be told. But then she went on the computer and looked it up, and she said you were right, they can live to be a lot older than what we think Jim is. Ainsley reminded me you're a veterinarian, after all, and said I should assume you know what you're talking about, which, okay, I can't see how I can argue with her there. Anyway, I couldn't stop thinking about whether it might be possible, and so I decided to poke around in the attic to see if I could find anything from my great-grandparents' time."

"You have things that old on your farm?" Someone really should encourage people to clean out their attics and donate anything historical to the museum. Somewhere to keep all those valuable old records that apparently just lay around Yorkshire basements and attics.

"Oh, sure. Lots of places around here have tons of historical stuff hanging around. You don't have boxes of old papers and whatnot from generations past in your attic?"

"I suppose I do." She should probably go through all the things up there and see what was what.

"With that old farm you inherited, I bet you've got lots of treasures."

"You might be right," Harriet said. "But what did you find?"

"I found a box of old household ledgers and journals, if you can believe it. Just about turned to dust, they were, but they held together well enough that I could look through them and see that they were written by my great-grandmother Mathilda. She was from Germany, originally. My sister Tilly was named after her. I never knew her, but my dad remembered her, and he said she was a tough one. Rarely cracked a smile, didn't put up with any nonsense, that kind of thing. Anyway, she kept track of every cent they ever spent on the farm in those ledgers, and from the looks of it, she never met a penny she wanted to let go of. Probably I should be grateful to her. It's her thriftiness that allowed them to save up enough to buy the back acreage."

"She sounds like she was a strong woman," Harriet said.

"She was something," Rupert said. "Anyway, Ainsley got interested and started looking through the journals to see if there was anything about Jim in there. And wouldn't you know it, she found a very interesting entry from January 1881. My great-grandmother recorded that her husband and oldest son went out to help clear the road to allow the lifeboat to be brought down from Whitby."

"You found an entry about the rescue of the *Visiter*?" Harriet asked.

"I guess so," Rupert said. "Crazy, isn't it?"

"It's crazy, and it's important. An actual first-person account of that night, from someone who was there? Historians would be all over that. You really might want to think about putting the journals in a museum, or a library somewhere."

"No one would want these old dusty things," Rupert said.

She was sure he was wrong, but she wasn't going to argue with him about it. Instead, she said, "What an incredible find. And your ancestors must have been really generous people to help out like that."

"I can't even imagine trying to clear away eight feet of snow so that a lifeboat could be brought down over these roads. It sounds like madness. But they made it."

"Thanks in part due to your great-grandfather," Harriet said.

"Well, anyway, it was the entry that followed two days after that one that caught Ainsley's attention."

"Why? What did it say?"

"How about you come by and take a look?"

As curious as Harriet was to see what Rupert had found in the journal, she told him it would have to wait until first thing the next day. She had a waiting room full of patients, and Will was meeting her at two thirty to drive to Hull, so she wouldn't have time to drive out to his farm and see the diary today. He said she was welcome to stop by any time the next day, and she promised she would come out and see him after she closed up the clinic at noon.

She spent the next few hours seeing patients, with a quick break for lunch, and they were ready to close up shop soon after two. Polly tidied up her desk while Harriet swept the waiting room floor.

"Right on time," Polly said as the door opened and Van stepped inside. Harriet thought about how sweet it was that Van was willing to ferry Polly to and from work. She could ride her bike, but she didn't always have the time, and it was nice how Van went so far out of his way to help her out.

"Hey, Polly, you ready?" Van asked. "I've got to drop you off and get back in time for a meeting with DI McCormick in a few."

"Sounds like something big is happening." Polly shut down her computer and started gathering her things.

"I wouldn't say that." Van hesitated and looked over at Harriet. "I just have some info for them."

Harriet stopped sweeping. "Info?"

"I asked about the footage from the harbor master's office," Van said. "From late Saturday night, early Sunday morning."

"What does it show?" Harriet asked.

"Nothing. They run their cameras on a one-hundred-twenty-hour loop. The Bellinghams went missing on Saturday night, and this is Friday. That footage has already been recorded over."

"Oh no." Harriet's heart sank. "So we don't know whether Shane is telling the truth or not."

"If you'd asked me a year ago, there wouldn't have been any doubt in my mind. I'd have said he was lying. But now, I don't know. He really does seem to have changed."

"I agree. I really think he's left that life behind," Harriet said. She didn't want to believe that Shane had lied.

"I'm sure the inspector will want to talk to Shane herself. If he's lying, she'll get it out of him. If not, she'll figure out what's really going on."

Harriet nodded. For now, it was time to get going if she and Will were driving to Hull and back. She could see him pulling into the driveway, returning from church.

"Will you let me know what happens?" she asked.

After a beat, Van said, "I'll share what I can."

Harriet thanked him, put the broom away, and then took Maxwell, Charlie, and Mercedes into the house. A few minutes later, she and Will were on their way to Hull. Harriet was glad he was the one driving. She was pretty much used to driving on the left side of the road by now, but sometimes it still threw her off, and she didn't mind sitting back and relaxing as the rolling hills flew past. There were no highways in this part of the country, so the drive took them past farms surrounded by fields and through villages with narrow roads. Several times they had to stop and wait for a car coming the other way, as the road wasn't always wide enough for two cars to pass at the same time.

"This Anthony guy sold Annie and Paul the sailboat, but the check didn't clear, and in the meantime, they managed to sail it away," Will said. "In this day and age, with so many ways to pay people instantly, I want to understand how that happened."

"That's why I want to talk to him," Harriet said "To see if he can explain. We know he showed up in Whitby, trying to get his boat back. And according to Eli, he was really vocal about it."

"Understandably. They stole his boat, which was worth at least a hundred thousand quid."

The buildings along the side of the road grew closer together as they approached the outskirts of Hull. The town was gathered along the banks of the Humber River, and a stunning modern bridge crossed the span. They followed their GPS to the neighborhood where Anthony lived, a section of the city with broad tree-lined streets and beautiful Victorian homes. Harriet recognized Anthony's house from the photos in the house tour article.

Will let out a low whistle as he parked. "Not bad," he said.

"I suppose if you can afford a fifty-foot sailboat, it's not surprising you'd have a big house," Harriet said.

"You're right about that," Will said. "So, we're just going to go to the door and see if he's home and ask to talk to him about his boat?"

"That's what I was thinking," Harriet said.

"I was kind of hoping there was more of a plan."

Now that he said it, she realized she wished she had more of a plan too. But she didn't want to admit it. "I promise, this usually works."

"You're cute and nonthreatening. People trust you instinctively."

"You need to make yourself look nonthreatening too, I guess." Then Harriet had an idea. "Do you have a clerical collar with you? You could put that on." He usually carried a spare in his car in case he needed it for hospital visits or other unexpected calls.

Will looked down at his blue-and-white checked shirt. "Great idea. I have a shirt and collar here somewhere. Hang on." He rummaged around in the back seat and found what he needed. It only took him a few moments to change.

"Much better," Harriet said. "No one's going to mess with a minister and his wife."

Will followed her up the path to Anthony's front door. She rang the doorbell and heard him take a deep breath beside her.

"Hello?" A woman blinked at them as she opened the door. "Can I help you?"

"We're so sorry to bother you," Will said. "I'm Will Knight, and this is my wife, Harriet. We're from White Church Bay, and we were hoping to speak with Anthony about his sailboat."

"His old sailboat, you mean," she said. "The one those hucksters stole from him?"

"That's the one," Harriet said. "We're trying to find those hucksters and thought maybe Anthony might be able to help us track them down."

"In that case, I'm sure he'd love to talk to you. He's all in a tizzy about that boat, let me tell you. But he's not here. He headed straight to the pub after he was done at the office. They're showing the footie match there."

"Football? On a Friday?" Will said.

"He likes Barcelona. Don't ask me why. I've been trying to figure it out for over thirty years. Can't root for Hull City like a normal person. Anyway, they're showing it at the pub, so that's where he is."

"Which pub is that?"

"The Donkey's Head, over on Chanterlands. You'll find him there."

Harriet was even more grateful to have Will along as they walked away from the house. "That was about soccer, right?"

"Football. And yes. He roots for Barcelona." Will consulted a map on his phone and pointed them in the right direction.

"I got that."

"That's not in the English system."

"Yes, I got that as well," Harriet said. "Even this American knows Barcelona's in Spain."

They found the pub easily enough, and when they made their way inside, they found the tables were full of people eating and chatting. A screen at the back of the room showed a soccer—football—match, and a dozen or so men stood around, looking up at the screen.

Harriet picked out Anthony without any trouble, recognizing the mostly bald head and the glasses. "That's him," she said. "In the button-down." He wore dark trousers and a light blue shirt rolled up at the sleeves, in contrast to the blue and red jerseys that most of the men watching the screen sported. She made her way to the rear of the pub.

"Anthony Maglione?" Harriet asked as she approached him. He nodded, sizing her up, and then glanced at Will.

"You must be the rector and wife. The missus texted me you were on your way here to talk to me. She said you're trying to find the thieves who stole my boat?"

"That's right," Will said.

"I already spoke to the police about this at length, both here in Hull and in Whitby. The police in Whitby questioned me about the fact that those thieves have gone missing. I don't know anything about that, if that's what you've come to find out."

"We're not with the police," Harriet said. "We're the ones who found the boat floating on the water on the coast of White Church Bay, so we're naturally quite curious about the whole situation."

Anthony nodded. "From what I understand, she likely would have smashed up against the rocks if you hadn't found her when you did," he said.

"We're just glad we did," Will said. "She's a beautiful boat."

That seemed to do the trick.

"Right. Come over here. It's quieter over in this corner." Anthony led them to a booth at a distance from the hubbub. "You guys want anything?"

"I could take a soda," Harriet said. Will went to the bar, came back with two sodas, and sat down on the bench next to Harriet.

"We're interested in hearing about how you ended up selling the boat to Annie and Paul," Harriet said.

"Not sure it's fair to say I sold it when I never did get my money, but okay. The story's pretty simple, really. I've had the *Salacia* for over twenty years. I bought her new, after I started my own practice, and I've loved her since the day I laid eyes on her. But I'm getting older now, and the kids are grown and don't come around all that often, and we just weren't using her all that much. I didn't want to give her up, but boats are expensive, what with the mooring and the upkeep and the gas and whatnot. My wife was getting frustrated. She wants a house in the country, you see. I keep telling her we don't need a house in the country because we can go anywhere with a boat, but she wasn't having it. Our oldest is about to have a baby, and she has her heart set on a place where we can all go and spend the holidays together. We went back and forth for a while, but you know how it goes when you're married. I want one thing, she wants another, and we compromise and do whatever she wants."

He grinned, and Harriet felt a stab of guilt. In just the last five days, she and Will had clashed over dishes in the sink, when to have guests over, and whether or not she should confront Anthony. In each situation, Will had yielded to her wishes and way of doing things. Harriet had heard the saying "Happy wife, happy life," but she determined right then and there that she wouldn't make Will live that way.

"So I listed the boat for sale—"

Harriet shook herself out of her reverie. "Where do you list a sailboat like that?" she asked. "Not on Craigslist, I assume?"

"No." Anthony laughed. "There are sites for this kind of thing. Yacht World, places like that. So I listed the *Salacia* and put up pictures, and it wasn't long at all before this couple reached out to me and said they were interested in buying it. They were from London, and they came out to see it, and they were so charming. Just, you know, well-dressed, said all the right things. Except they didn't tell me they were Paul and Annie Bellingham. They said their names were Spencer and Stephanie Duncan."

Harriet looked at Will and could tell he was as startled as she was at this bit of information. It hadn't even occurred to her that Paul and Annie had used fake names to steal the boat.

"They said they were selling their home and wanted to travel around the country and have an adventure," Anthony continued. "It was exactly what I wanted to do when I was their age, only I was too chicken to chuck it all, but here they were, actually doing it. I was impressed, and it just felt right, so I said great. We agreed on a price and shook on it. They said they were waiting on a check from the sale of their house, and that it would happen very soon. They were anxious to get going, but they promised me they would have the money within a week. They would write me a check as soon as it came in."

"You didn't require a certified check?" For that much money, Harriet thought he would have insisted on proof that the cash was in the account.

"I was planning to, but they talked again about how it would slow things down and they were anxious to get going. I know now I was foolish, but they were about our kids' ages, and I knew that if they were in this young couple's shoes, I would want someone to trust them. To give them a chance at their dreams. So I did. Against all reason, I let them take the boat. They handed me a post-dated personal check and promised to let me know when the money was in the account, and I gave them the keys to the *Salacia*. They sailed her away the next day, and that was that."

Anthony took in a deep breath and let it out slowly. "I should have done more research. I should have seen it coming. I should have—I don't even know. I was just too trusting I guess."

"That's not a terrible personality trait," Harriet said.

"I should have known better, shouldn't I, though?" Anthony said. "I was swept up in the adventure of it all. And they were so posh, talking about how she'd grown up sailing with her grandfather, and she let slip something about her trust fund, and I just... I fell for it, hook, line, and sinker."

"They've managed to fool a lot of people, judging from what we've seen," Harriet said.

"You reported them at the time, right?" Will asked, though Harriet knew he knew the answer.

"I did. I told the police the registration number of the boat, and they assured me they'd get an alert out to marinas to be on the lookout for it." He frowned. "When I went to the Whitby marina day before yesterday, they discovered that someone had transposed two of the numbers, so they were all looking for the wrong boat."

"I noticed that you commented on a couple of their videos," Harriet said. "How did you find out who they really were?"

"My daughter called me last week and told me she'd seen my boat on a video. She got a real good look at it and recognized it right away. She sent me a link, and as soon as I saw their profile picture, I knew these were the people who'd stolen my boat. That's when I went back to the police in Hull. Then I started watching their videos, getting angrier and angrier with each one. They sure made it seem like they had a nice life, didn't they? So much money, so much class."

"They had a lot of people fooled," Harriet said again sympathetically.

"You figured out it was me who left those comments, did you?" He took a long drink from his glass. "I wasn't so subtle, I guess."

"AnthonyMag as your screen name was kind of a giveaway," Harriet told him.

"Yeah, well, I wasn't trying to hide anything. I wanted them to know I was onto them. I wanted them to know I was tracking them and they hadn't gotten away with it."

"I didn't see that they ever responded," Harriet said.

"What were they going to do, admit that they were actually big fakes? Not likely. Of course they just ignored my messages," Anthony said. "But once I figured out they were putting their route on the internet, telling the whole world where they were going, I went a couple of places, hoping to catch them."

"You went to meet them?" Harriet asked.

"Sure. But they never showed. I think they must have gone to the places they said they went to, obviously, because they filmed it, but I don't think they were always in those places when they said they were."

"And so you were upset," Will said.

"Of course I was upset. They owed me a hundred and twenty thousand quid. Not only that, I loved that boat. I thought I was selling the *Salacia* to a nice couple who wanted a big adventure. But they're not a nice couple. They're con artists, both of them. I never would have let go of the boat if I'd known. Then earlier this week I saw a picture of the *Salacia* in the paper, and about Paul and Annie Bellingham going missing, and I knew. I just knew."

"Knew what?" Harriet asked.

"That they're conning someone else."

"Who are they conning, do you think?"

"I don't know," he said. "Me, maybe. They knew I was going to catch up with them, so they found a way to escape without having to face the consequences. Or, who knows, maybe I wasn't the only one they've conned. Probably I wasn't. I bet they owe money all over the place. So maybe they made it look like something terrible happened and they used it as an opportunity to escape. Start over."

"One theory about what happened is exactly as you say," Will said. "That they disappeared on purpose for some reason. But there's another theory floating around out there."

"What's that?"

"Another theory is that someone with bad intentions boarded the boat."

"You think someone kidnapped them? Like they're some children on a milk carton? Is there a ransom note? Because if there is, the kidnapper's barking up the wrong tree. No one's going to offer a red cent to get them back. That's what I told the police when they asked me about it."

"The police asked you about their disappearance?"

"Yeah, like I said, they talked to me about it after I showed up in Whitby. Apparently, that made me a 'person of interest,' whatever that means. But I had an ironclad alibi for when they disappeared, so that was too bad for them."

"What was your alibi?" Will asked.

"You don't think I had something to do with it too, do you?" He leaned forward in his chair.

"We're just trying to establish that you *couldn't* have had anything to do with it," Will said smoothly, and the words seemed to calm Anthony down. "Don't worry. Neither of us thinks you had anything to do with it."

Harriet wasn't entirely sure that was completely true, but the words had the intended effect. "Good. Because I didn't. I'll tell you what I told the police. The last time I saw those two thieves was when I handed them the keys. And during the timeframe when they could have disappeared, I was doing open-heart surgery. Dozens of witnesses—nurses, techs, the patient's family—can all vouch for me being at the hospital all weekend."

"That seems pretty ironclad," Harriet said. "Then, can you tell me, since you interacted with them, do you think there's any chance someone could have done more than kidnapped them?"

"You think someone *killed* them?" he said. To his credit, he seemed genuinely distressed by the thought. "Do you think they made the wrong person mad? Like I said, it couldn't have been just me they ripped off. Surely there were other people after them too. Do you actually think—"

It seemed that he didn't know how to finish that sentence.

"We really don't know. Obviously, we hope not," Harriet said.

"I mean, I guess it's possible, but that's terrible to even consider."

"I totally agree," Will said. "Let's hope that's not it." He took a sip of his soda. "You said you were trying to track Annie and Paul down. Did you have access to the boat's location data?"

"Not after I gave them the boat. If I had, it would have been easy to find them, wouldn't it? Even when they weren't where they said they would be. I would have loved to have seen them again."

"That makes several of us who have been trying to find them, and failing," Harriet said, shaking her head.

There was a beat of silence. Then the pub erupted, and Anthony threw his arms into the air and started shouting along with everyone else.

"Score for Barcelona," Will said. She'd assumed as much. She hadn't realized that from where Anthony sat he could still see the TV. When he finally put his arms down and turned back to them, Harriet had a question ready.

"You said you went to the Whitby marina two days ago," she said.

"That's right." He took a drink from his glass again. "At the end of the day, I just want the *Salacia* back. I was hoping the Coastguard would release her to me. But they wouldn't."

"I imagine it's still evidence in an active investigation," Harriet said. "But perhaps once they've got it all settled."

"Let's hope so," Anthony said.

Harriet took a deep breath and then said, "Annie's and Paul's phones went missing when they did. You believe they wanted to disappear on purpose, and it makes sense that they would take their phones with them, in that case, doesn't it?"

"Yeah. People take their phones everywhere these days, don't they?" Anthony said. "Makes sense."

"Their phones have been turned off for nearly the entire time they've been missing," Will said.

Anthony nodded. "That makes sense too, I guess. If they wanted to disappear, they wouldn't want their phones to be trackable."

"Like Will said, their phones have been off for almost the whole time they've been missing," Harriet said. "But one of them was turned on, briefly, on Wednesday. It hit a cell tower in Whitby."

"Whoa." He set his glass down a little too hard. "They were in Whitby? Just two days ago?"

"They were, or their phones were," Harriet said.

Anthony stared at her, frowning. "No," he said. "Look, if you're trying to imply that I might have their phones, or hurt them in some way…" He shook his head. "Okay, I guess I can see why you would think that from the comments I left."

"You sounded really angry," Harriet said. "Understandably so."

"They bilked you out of a hundred thousand pounds," Will added.

"A hundred and twenty," Anthony said. "But if that's what you came here to find out, the answer is no. I was angry—still am—and I want to see them punished for what they've done. But I don't want to see them dead. I don't want to see them hurt. I don't want them to be lost on the North Sea in a life raft. I don't have their mobiles, and I don't know where they are. I had nothing to do with them going missing."

"What do you think happened to them?" Harriet asked.

Anthony sat back in his chair and stretched his legs out in front of him, crossing one over the other. "Like I said, I think they disappeared on purpose. It's the only thing that makes sense. They weren't lost in a storm. They weren't swept overboard. They saw a chance to make their escape, and they did. They didn't care about the *Salacia*.

They just left her floating on the sea. They don't care about anything but themselves and making money with their video channel."

Harriet thought about what he was saying, thought about all the clues they'd come up with so far, and realized he was probably right. She thought there was a decent chance the Bellinghams really did disappear on purpose.

It didn't solve the mystery, even if it was true, but talking with Anthony made her realize that it probably was the most likely scenario.

"Thank you for talking with us," Will said, holding out his hand. "We'll let you get back to your game."

Anthony shook it and nodded at Will and then Harriet. "I hope you find them. Not just so I can get the *Salacia* back, though I really do want that too. But they need to be found. They need to be brought to justice."

"We'll keep you posted if we learn anything about where they went off to," Harriet said.

"Thank you."

"He wasn't what I expected," Will said as soon as they were back in the car.

"What did you expect?"

"Somewhere between an enraged theft victim and a homicidal maniac, I guess," Will said. "But it turns out he's just a regular guy."

"A guy who's really upset about a boat."

"A guy who trusted two people and watched them stomp all over that trust. Who lost a lot of money by taking people at their word and having them turn on him."

"A guy who lovingly refers to his boat as 'she,'" Harriet said. "Maybe that's just old-fashioned and charming though?"

"It's a funny name, isn't it?" Will mused as he drove through the streets of Hull, heading to the road that would lead north and back home. "The *Salacia*? The Roman goddess of the sea. It's quite a grand name. A lot to live up to, if you ask me. It's kind of like naming your kid Trinity. Like, that's a lot of pressure."

"Salacia is the goddess of the sea?" Harriet had never really paid that much attention to mythology. She couldn't keep straight who was supposed to be in charge of what.

"In Roman mythology, sure. The goddess of salt water, which sounds less impressive than the goddess of the sea, if you ask me. They believed she presided over the depths of the ocean. It's interesting how back then people believed in so many different gods for different parts of their lives. What a mind shift it must have been when the ancient Israelites showed up with their talk of Yahweh, the One True God. If you've spent your whole life thinking there are hundreds of gods, an idea like that would be hard to get your head around."

As much as Harriet enjoyed Will's musings—and she really did, she loved that he was curious about other cultures' beliefs and customs, and she was grateful to be married to someone who cared about everyone else's feelings, even the feelings of the ancient Romans—she was still stuck on the news about Salacia.

"Why have I never heard of Salacia, the goddess of the sea? She wasn't one of their major gods?"

"Probably because she's overshadowed by her husband, Neptune. He's much more well known than she is."

"Neptune?" Her stomach dropped, and her heartbeat sped up. She could hear blood rushing in her ears. "Salacia is married to Neptune?"

"Yeah." He turned his head and looked at her. "Why are you staring at me like that?"

That message board. The message posted by someone named Neptune, asking for a favor from someone in the Whitby area. What if Paul and Annie used the name Neptune because they were on a boat named Salacia?

"I have to call Van."

CHAPTER NINETEEN

When Harriet and Will got back home, Harriet let the dogs out and Will said he was going to make dinner again and that she should relax.

"I stopped at the store on my way home earlier this morning," he said. "I picked up ingredients for another run at my famous chicken and rice."

"Did you get a new fire extinguisher while you're at it?" Harriet teased.

"I won't need a fire extinguisher so long as a certain pretty woman doesn't distract me this time. Go relax. You did good work today."

Harriet was glad to take him up on it. There were plenty of things she wanted to do. Where to start? She wanted to get through videos and comments on Annie and Paul's page to see if there were any clues hidden there that might point to what happened to them. She wanted to call Van and see if the officers had looked at the message boards and figured out who Nessie was yet, or why one of the phones had turned on, or where Annie and Paul were. She was itchy with questions and feelings and confusion, and she didn't think she would be able to sit still for very long, so she decided to get outside.

"In that case, I think I'm going for a walk," she said.

"That sounds like an excellent idea," Will said. "Enjoy."

She grabbed her jacket, headed for the door, and made her way to the cliffs, once again drawn by the promise of the view of the bay. But she only made it as far as Aunt Jinny's garden.

"Well, hello," her aunt said, smiling as Harriet approached. "Enjoying the night?"

"I sometimes wonder if you ever stop working in your garden," Harriet said.

"Not if I can help it." Aunt Jinny grinned and held up a wicker basket. "I'm harvesting green beans."

"That's fun. Did you get a lot?"

"Not a lot, but enough. Which is the perfect amount."

"I suppose it is." Harriet wished she could channel some of Aunt Jinny's calm right about now. Her aunt never seemed to get flustered. "How are you?"

"I'm doing okay. Can't complain." She reached out and pulled off a long green bean and dropped it in the basket. "And you? How's Will?"

"Currently making dinner for me."

"He's a keeper," Aunt Jinny said. "It's nice to see how young men these days can be willing to split the housework, and even childcare, when the time comes."

"He's pretty great." Harriet agreed.

"But...?"

"But what?"

"There was a *but* coming."

"No there wasn't." Was there?

Aunt Jinny didn't say anything for a moment, she just watched Harriet. After a few moments, her unblinking gaze made Harriet squirm.

"But I guess we're still figuring things out," Harriet finally said.

"Go on." Aunt Jinny set her basket down on a little bench inside the garden.

"Like, yesterday I nearly lost it with him because he'd made this elaborate breakfast, which was fine, even though I'd really just wanted a quick breakfast and time to read my Bible. But whatever, I'm not going to complain about bacon. But then he left dirty dishes in the sink all day, and I saw it, and he knows I hate it when dirty dishes are left in the sink—"

"And it felt like he didn't care about your feelings."

"I—" Harriet broke off, processing her aunt's words. "Yeah, I guess that's it. It wasn't so much the dirty dishes that bothered me, it was the fact that I'd told him I hated it, and he did it anyway, and yeah, I guess you're right, it made me feel like he just didn't care about my feelings."

"Did you tell him?"

"I was about to, but then I came home and he'd cleaned up the kitchen. And then he apologized for leaving them there earlier. He'd had to go to the deathbed of a parishioner, which is about as good an excuse as you can get, but after that he cleaned them up before I got home. And then I felt like a total jerk for being angry about it all day."

"It sounds like he had a good reason, so I suppose you can't fault him for that, but that doesn't mean your feelings aren't valid," Aunt Jinny said. "Those are still real, and they need to be dealt with."

"I don't know how to deal with them."

"Acknowledging them is a good first step. You felt hurt because you thought Will didn't care about your feelings. Of course that made you angry. Only a few weeks ago, he pledged to love and honor you, and it felt to you like he wasn't doing that. There's nothing wrong with admitting that." She pulled one gardening glove off and then the other and set them on top of the beans in the basket. "And then, yes, maybe try to give him the benefit of the doubt, at least until you have a chance to talk with him about it and hear what's going on with him and listen to his feelings."

His feelings. Right. She'd been so concentrated on her own that she hadn't asked about his. She thought about the decision she'd made just a few hours ago, not to insist on her way all the time. It was only fair that she defer to his traditions and habits once in a while.

"You're learning to live with each other," Aunt Jinny said. "After living alone for years. It's a huge adjustment, for both of you."

"This is what I wanted for so long though," Harriet said. "I feel guilty that I'm not blissful every moment of every day. That's what being a newlywed is supposed to be like, right?"

"Ha! Maybe in the movies. Certainly not in real life," Aunt Jinny said. "I don't think Dom and I ever fought as much in all the years of our marriage as we did that first year. It didn't mean we didn't love each other. Just that we were figuring out how to live together. Having feelings doesn't mean you don't love Will. It means you have to work together to figure out how you're going to build your lives. It's not always easy, but it is worth it. Will's a good man. A great man. But he's not perfect. And neither, my dear, are you."

Harriet smiled at that. Of course she wasn't.

"But you love each other, and you love the Lord, and you're committed to making it work, and that's the most important thing."

"Thank you, Aunt Jinny." She smiled.

"Even with the hard patches, I wouldn't trade one day of my many years with Dominic. Do your best to enjoy it, Harriet."

The tears that welled up in Aunt Jinny's eyes made it clear that more than a decade after Uncle Dominic passed, Aunt Jinny still missed him. Harriet didn't know what it was like to spend decades with someone and then lose them. It sounded terrible. Like losing an arm. The thought of losing Will—she wasn't sure she would survive it. She hoped they both lived a very long time.

Will served a delicious dinner of slightly undercooked rice and overdone chicken. Harriet had seconds, thanked him for cooking, and then they cleaned up the kitchen together. Harriet enjoyed the time with him, even while her hands were plunged in hot soapy water. Not every guy would be joking around with her while drying dishes, and even though every moment wasn't going to be perfect, they were in it for the long haul, and she was glad to have Will by her side.

She slept fitfully that night, her mind still swirling with thoughts about Annie and Paul and Shane O'Grady and Anthony Maglione. She couldn't shake the sense that she was missing something. That the answer to what happened to the boaters was right there in front of her, but she just wasn't seeing it.

She rose early, brewed a pot of coffee, and spent some time reading her Bible before she put on her jacket and headed for her car. Will was still sleeping, no doubt with Ash curled up beside him, when she climbed into the Beast and headed for Rupert's farm. The roads were mostly empty, and the fields were covered with a gauzy mist that would burn off as the day heated up. But for now, a ghostly, otherworldly haze lay over the landscape. She pulled into the Bakers' driveway and found Rupert out by the llama pen. The llamas were grazing and didn't seem to notice as Harriet walked up, but she saw that Jim was next to Rupert, eating slices of apple and lettuce out of a plastic dish.

"Hello, Harriet." He turned to face her. "Thank you for coming out."

"Of course." She bent down to get a closer look at Jim. He really was a beautiful creature. She reached out and ran her fingers over the carvings in his shell. *J*, she felt. And then, *M*. There was no *I*. She felt the area again and then looked closer and saw that her earlier guess had been right. What looked like an *I* was a marking on the turtle's shell.

"It just says J-M," Harriet said. "Not J-I-M."

"Oh yeah, I know that," Rupert said. "But it looks like Jim, so that's what we've always called him."

James Merritt. The initials of the little boy who had received the tortoise as a Christmas gift while his parents were stationed in India.

"It stands for James Merritt."

"Who's that?"

"A little boy who carved his initials into Jim's shell almost a hundred and fifty years ago." That boy no doubt grew up and went on to have children, grandchildren, and great-grandchildren. How many generations had this tortoise outlived? It was crazy to think how much had happened since Jim washed up on shore. How much the world had changed.

But not only that, it was a stark reminder that life—human life, anyway—was short and that she only had a few years left on this earth. She'd better use the time she had well.

"Did you want to see the journals then?" Rupert asked.

"Please."

He gestured for her to follow him and started walking to the house. The stone cottage had two stories and a steeply pitched roof, and the house and yard were surrounded by a white fence covered in climbing roses and morning glories. He led her through the back door, and they were greeted by the smell of fresh-baked bread and sausage. Rupert called out, "The vet's here."

The room was warm and snug, with whitewashed walls and the low ceilings that said this farmhouse was very old. A stack of leather-bound journals sat on a wooden table.

"Oh, hello, Dr. Bailey." A woman—Ainsley, Harriet assumed—walked toward them, wiping her hands on a floral apron. She had wispy white hair pulled back into a bun and big blue eyes. "Rupert told me you think Old Jim is *really* old. Old enough to have been on that shipwreck from the 1880s."

"He is," Harriet said. "He started out in the Seychelles Islands in the late 1870s and then went to India for a few years before coming here."

"So you're telling me that not only is Jim older than I am, but he's seen more of the world too?"

Harriet laughed. "You and me both, I'm afraid."

"Rupert brought down these old journals, and I started paging through them, looking for, I don't even know what, really. But I found this." Ainsley picked up the journal on top and opened to a page she'd marked with a scrap of paper. She handed it to Harriet.

Harriet worried she should be wearing gloves to protect the pages but took the journal anyway.

"The entry starts on that page," Ainsley said, pointing to the right side. Harriet squinted at the spidery handwriting. Between the faded ink and the stained pages, it was hard to discern, but she could just make out the words.

> *January 18, 1881*
> *Howard still has chills, but he's feeling much better. I tried to get him to stay in bed, but he would not. After chores this morning he went down to the beach because he heard from Lucas Pettigrew that things were washing up from the ship. Lucas said Henry Graham found a sapphire necklace tangled in the seaweed, but I can't believe that. Still, Howard would not be left out, so off he went. He came back not with sapphires but with a turtle. I don't know what we're going to do with a turtle, but he is a cute little thing, about the size of my forearm, and Howard says we're keeping him. That man would take in every stray he came across if I let him. The tortoise has a J and an M on his shell, so Howard says his name is Jim.*

The entry went on from there, but this was what Harriet needed. An explanation for how the tortoise got from the beaches of Africa to a farm in East Yorkshire.

"Jim must have been quite young at the time, if he was only the size of a forearm," Harriet said. "Which helps explain why he's still around today."

"I bet they were surprised to see how big their cute little tortoise got," Rupert said, smiling.

"I'm sure they didn't know what they were in for when they took him home," Harriet said. "But your family has done a wonderful job of caring for him over the years."

"He's part of the family," Ainsley said. "A weird, lumbering part of the family, that also includes a herd of llamas, but a family nonetheless."

Harriet handed the journal back to Ainsley. "Thank you for sharing that with me. I'm glad to know what really happened."

"It's funny, isn't it?" Rupert said. "I had no idea Jim was something of a celebrity."

"He's got a fascinating story, that's for sure." Harriet smiled. "And if you keep taking such good care of him, he might live for many more years."

Harriet walked to her car, marveling at the story. It was good to know how Jim had ended up on a farm in Yorkshire. It was good to finally have answers.

She headed back to the clinic. Now, if only she could say the same for the mystery of the missing boaters.

CHAPTER TWENTY

After Harriet got back to the office, she spent the next couple of hours seeing patients, but even as she cuddled kittens and comforted scared dogs, she thought about all that had happened in the past few days, trying to make sense of the clues that rattled around in her mind. Annie and Paul were still missing. They were out there somewhere—possibly in Whitby, or at least one of their phones was in Whitby recently. Three days before they went missing, they'd posted a message on a local chat board, asking for help.

After she closed up the office and sent Polly home, she returned to the house, sat down on the couch, and opened her laptop. Will was playing tennis with one of the guys in his Bible study, and she didn't think he would be back for another hour or so. She would use this time to try to figure out what it was that was bothering her.

There was something she was missing, she was sure of it. There had to be something that would point her to what really happened. She just had this sense that it was there, right in front of her, but she didn't see it. She went back to Annie and Paul's video channel and poked around. There were several videos she hadn't yet seen. She clicked on one, about a stop they made at an island called Lindisfarne, or Holy Island. It was located just below the English border with Scotland, had several historic churches and an abandoned monastery, and was known as a pilgrimage site. It was a darling little place, with a town only a few blocks wide and a few blocks long, with dramatic scenery beyond and a rich liturgical history. It looked fascinating, and it was only a couple hours' drive from White Church Bay. Maybe she could convince Will that they should check it out sometime. But if there was a clue in this video, she didn't see it.

The next one in the series was another DISASTER! video, this time about a mishap with a split hose that meant the boat was taking on water. Just how many things could go wrong on a sailboat? It was enough to make her never want to set foot on a boat again. She wondered once more, were they just particularly unlucky, or was this number of sailing mishaps normal? Harriet noticed again something she'd picked up on before—the disaster videos had more views and comments than the videos that simply showed the couple wandering around the small towns. Way more.

"Hey, sweetheart!" Will came in and set his tennis racket and gym bag down just inside the door. He looked genuinely delighted to see her, and her heart melted a little. "How's it going? You look like you're deep in thought."

"I'm trying to figure out if Annie and Paul manufactured disasters as they sailed so they could post videos about them."

"Interesting idea. What makes you say that?"

Harriet gestured for him to come see, and when he sat beside her, she scrolled down the page, pointing out the disaster videos. "See, here's the first one that they call DISASTER! But it's just a video about how they forgot to latch the cabinet doors, so they opened and things spilled. Not exactly a disaster. But see how many more views this video got than the one before it?" She scrolled back to the video about the town of Padstowe and pointed at the number below it. "And then here's the next disaster video. This one's about how they forgot to empty their toilet tank, and it got nearly twice as many views as the cabinet one. It's way more than the travelogue videos. And with each subsequent disaster video, the problems get more dramatic and the number of views goes up. Here they nearly blew up their boat, and in this one, they claim to have just escaped sinking it, and in this one, they almost ran aground. All of the 'disaster' videos have a ton of views."

"Wow."

"Is it possible for one couple to have so many accidents?"

"I suppose so, if they're actually just extremely inexperienced or incompetent. But based on what you've shown me of their videos, they're neither."

"No," Harriet said. "In fact, the sense I'm getting is that they're very canny."

"They know exactly what they're doing."

"The more views a video gets, the more views the ads at the beginning get," Harriet said. "I'm not the most savvy person when it comes to these things, but it only makes sense that the more views the ads get, the more compensation Annie and Paul get. So they're incentivized to keep coming up with bigger and bigger disasters to keep the viewers coming back."

"Oh." Will's eyes widened. "So that could be a motive..."

"I don't know," Harriet said. She thought about something Mrs. Lewis had said, something she'd completely dismissed at the time. "Mrs. Lewis said her daughter suggested that they disappeared as part of a publicity stunt."

"Making it look like you've been swept overboard is a pretty big disaster," Will said. "It could get you a lot of publicity."

"It *has* gotten them a lot of publicity. And a huge number of views on their videos."

"But even if that's what's going on here—and it's a very big if—how would it work? I mean, it's now been almost a week since we found the sailboat. Where have they been? Are they planning to suddenly reappear and make people think they've been lost at sea all this time?"

"No one's going to believe that," Harriet said. "No way they could have survived this long in a raft. Especially with Paul's diabetes—it would be very foolish of him to take a chance like that."

"But they're not out on a raft lost at sea. They tried to make it look like that, but we're nearly sure it's not the case, right?"

"Right. So where are they?"

Harriet had an idea. "Shane."

"Shane? What about him?"

She thought back over the interactions she'd had with him the past few days. She closed her eyes and tried to picture the scene at the marina.

"Do you remember when we saw him Sunday afternoon?"

"I remember he was carrying bags of fast food. That chicken smelled really good."

"Was he carrying more food than was needed for one person?"

"Maybe he was hungry."

"When I saw him again on Thursday, he was coming off his boat with a trash bag. Inside were more takeaway bags and cartons."

"He's a single guy. Can't blame him for liking fast food."

Maybe it meant something, or maybe it didn't.

"Shane has been on the straight and narrow, Harriet. He wants to leave all that behind. I really don't think he would be involved in this."

Good, sweet, kind Will, who always saw the best in everybody. Maybe he was right. Maybe Shane had nothing to do with it. But she wouldn't solve this thing by closing her eyes to what was in front of her.

"What are you thinking, Harriet? What are you suggesting?"

"I don't know," she said, but even as she said the words, she realized they weren't true. "I guess I'm trying to figure out if Shane is Nessie."

"Nessie? The sea monster?"

"From the message board."

"Show me again?"

She pulled up the page and tried to find the thread she'd seen earlier in the week. But it was gone. The entire message thread started by Neptune had been deleted, including the answer from Nessie. "It's not here."

"What?"

"It's been deleted."

Will leaned forward. "Ah," he said. "That can't be an accident."

"No, I don't suppose it is," Harriet said. "But now what?"

"We find a different way to figure this out," Will said. "How else can we tell if Shane is Nessie?"

Harriet typed the name *Shane O'Grady* into the search bar and hit return. She didn't know what she was looking for. He wasn't going to have publicly posted something that implicated him as Nessie, or as being involved in this situation, or—

"What's that?" Will asked, pointing to a link on her screen.

"Mug shot," Harriet said, clicking on the link. "Looks like from when he was arrested for the fish tank thing." She had come across his mug shot before, when she was investigating the smuggling mystery. "I think it's unfortunate how high up in the search results that comes up, but people must click on it a lot."

"Look." Will pointed at the screen. "Look at his name."

"Shane Nestor O'Grady," Harriet said, and her mouth dropped open. "Nessie is short for Nestor. He's the sea monster."

"He could be," Will said. "We don't know for sure that he is."

But Harriet knew. She felt in her bones that Nessie was a name Shane had used that was taken from his middle name. That he'd responded to Annie and Paul's request for help. That they'd paid him to—

To what?

"He couldn't have done this," Will protested. "He wouldn't."

Harriet wanted to agree with him, but it was getting harder and harder to ignore the evidence.

"Do you think they paid him to help them disappear?" Harriet said. "They wanted to make it look like they were lost at sea. Swept overboard in a storm…"

"And they found someone to pick them up from their boat…"

"But where did he take them?" Harriet asked. Then she realized she knew the answer. "He didn't take them anywhere. They're on his boat in the marina in Whitby. They've been there this whole time."

"What makes you say that?"

"Just think about it. It probably wasn't Paul and Annie's original plan that they would be there so long, but his engine went out." It all started to take shape in her mind. "Their plan was probably to stay on his boat only a day or so, just long enough to make it convincing, and then have Shane drop them back in the water on the missing life raft. They could take a video from the raft and make it look like they'd been lost at sea the whole time. That's why they kept their phones with them, most likely—and they would have been spotted pretty quickly, since the Coastguard had every boat in the area out looking for them."

"The question is, how much of this did Shane know about?" Will said. "I want to believe he's an unsuspecting pawn."

"On paper, it would have sounded like a good plan," Harriet said. "Only, Shane couldn't get the part he needed for his boat, which meant that he was stuck in the marina. Annie and Paul have had to stay on his boat for almost a week, risking detection and killing all hope of plausibility for their story."

"And now the Coastguard has called off their search. So do you think they'll go through with their plan when Shane gets his boat fixed?"

"I have no idea how they're going to get out of this," Harriet said.

Will shook his head. "So they've been right there under the police's nose this whole time?"

"I believe it," Harriet said. "That's why one of their phones pinged a cell tower in Whitby when it was turned on. Because they were right there in Whitby Harbor."

"That's maybe why Shane had the fast food," Will said. "And the fast food trash."

"They're on Shane's boat," Harriet said. "I'm sure of it."

"Is there any way to prove it?" Will asked.

Neither of them spoke for a moment. There had to be a way. Couldn't they just go down to the marina and walk onto Shane's boat and find them? Or send the police again? Maybe she'd have to call Van. If they could get a warrant, Shane would have to let the police search the boat.

Will's phone rang, breaking her train of thought. Will pulled the phone out of his pocket and looked down.

"It's Kyle," he said.

Will answered the call and put the phone to his ear, but his volume was up high enough that Harriet could hear every word Kyle said.

"Hey, Will. I'm at the marina, getting my boat ready to go out fishing, and it may not be anything, but a little while ago, those three police officers all came down to talk to Shane O'Grady, but he was gone—"

"He's gone?"

"Yes, I saw his boat leave the dock a few minutes ago, and it's almost out of the harbor now."

"Thanks for calling, Kyle," Will said. "That's very good to know."

As soon as he hung up, he turned to Harriet. "Let's go."

CHAPTER TWENTY-ONE

Will threw on a sweatshirt and sweatpants over his shorts and T-shirt, and as they rushed to the car, Harriet called Van while Will called Eli. Both of them explained what was going on, and then Will slid behind the wheel and peeled out.

"The police are on their way to the marina," Harriet said. "They've got a boat tied up there."

"They'd better hurry if they're going to catch them," Will said. "Kyle is on his way out, trying to keep a visual on the boat, but Shane's boat is faster, so it'll be tough." He raced down the road, zooming past farmhouses and fields. "What do you think they're doing? Where are they headed?"

"It was just Shane's boat that left the marina?" Harriet asked. "Not the *Salacia*?"

"As far as I know, the sailboat is still tied up at the Coastguard dock in the marina."

She held on to the door handle as Will raced around a curve in the road. "I have no idea what kind of story they told him or what they're up to."

"Do you think they're fleeing the country?"

"I don't know," Harriet said. "It doesn't seem likely." It would be ironic if once again they were on the chase after a boat hoping to make it into international waters. "Maybe they're having him take them somewhere to drop them off at another boat."

"Even if they're running away, it doesn't seem likely he would be. Based on what we saw in that chat, he's not behind this in any way."

"He wouldn't have helped them just out of the goodness of his heart though."

"They paid him for his help, almost certainly," Will said. "But maybe he didn't realize what he was getting into. Maybe, with his mother's situation, helping them seemed like an easy way to get the cash he needed. But he wouldn't knowingly be an accomplice in their crimes or sign up for what this has become."

"And he certainly didn't know his boat was going to break down," Harriet said. "That's got to have thrown a wrench in their plan. So they were trapped in the harbor for far longer than they intended. Shane was supposed to get the part he needed yesterday, but maybe they didn't leave the moment the boat was ready to go. Maybe they were trying to come up with a new plan, since the possibility they were lost at sea all this time hardly seemed plausible."

They were getting close now. Only a few more blocks, and they would be there.

"So they're headed out to sea," Harriet said. "And then what?"

"I don't know," Will said. "But hopefully we'll catch them before anything happens."

"Will, it's not this way," Harriet said as he turned right, away from the marina. "You have to go that way to get to the marina."

"We're not going to the marina," Will said.

"Where are we going?"

"There." Up ahead was a large building surrounded by a tall fence with a blue sign that said HIS MAJESTY'S COASTGUARD.

"The Coastguard building?"

"There's a team already launched from the Coastguard dock at the marina," Will said. "But we're not taking a boat."

"Will, what are we doing?"

He slowed down as they approached a small security booth. "We're here for Eli Baine," he said to the guard at the window.

"Good to see you, Will," the man said, and waved them through. "Eli's waiting at the pad."

"Have a great day," Will called. He drove a few yards and then parked in a lot on the side of the building. "Come on, we'd better hurry."

Harriet scrambled out of the car and ran after Will as he jogged to a wide, flat area where a helicopter sat waiting, its rotor blades whirring.

"You're just in time," Eli called as he leaned out the open helicopter door.

"Just in time for what?" Harriet asked.

"You want to catch these guys, right?" Will said. "The best way to spot them is going to be from the air."

He couldn't be serious. They were really going to ride in a Coastguard helicopter? How could that happen? They couldn't just—

Will led her under the rotor, wind whipping her hair in every direction.

The Coastguard wouldn't let them—

He hopped into the open door of the helicopter.

She didn't want to—

But before she knew what was happening, Will was holding out his hand. "Come on!" he shouted.

"Is this allowed?" She also had to shout to be heard over the roar of the motor.

"I'm a Coastguard chaplain," he said. "They let me come along sometimes, remember?"

She thought that meant on, like, cruises around the bay. Not things like this. Not helicopters.

"You coming or not?" Eli yelled. "We've gotta go."

She glanced at Will, who grinned at her. "Let's go find them!" he shouted.

She reached out and took his hand.

CHAPTER TWENTY-TWO

Harriet barely had time to strap in before Eli took off and the helicopter rose into the sky. Officer Vasquez, the officer Harriet had met when they found the boat—was that really less than a week ago?—handed her a headset and showed her how to turn it on. The headphones blocked the sound of the motor and allowed her to hear what the others were saying.

"They were headed north," Eli said. "But they're so far ahead of the chaser boats that we're not sure where he is."

"Let's go get 'em," Will said.

Harriet grasped the handle on the side of her seat as the helicopter banked and turned to the north.

"First time?" Officer Vasquez asked.

Harriet shook her head. She'd had a short ride in a search and rescue helicopter a year ago when a friend was injured in a cave. She peered out the windows. The whole coast was spread out below them, the land green and lush until it gave way to reddish-brown cliffs and then the sparkling blue sea. She could see not only boats on the water, chugging toward and away from the marina and up and down the coast, but she also could see the people on the boats.

"I never tire of the view," Officer Vasquez said. "And we're in good hands. Baine is the best helicopter pilot we've got."

Harriet could see waves racing to shore. She could even make out what looked like the hull of an old boat along the shallow water in the north of the cove.

"Is that an old shipwreck?" She pointed to the dark shape in the water.

"Yep. That's the *Sarb-J*," Officer Vasquez said. "Sunk in 1994."

"Wow." It was incredible to be able to see the world from this angle.

"How did Shane get so far ahead of the other boats?" Will asked. "I thought Kyle was going to follow right after him?"

"Turns out Manning needed petrol," Eli said. "He couldn't get away from the marina without refilling his tank, and there was a wait. By the time he got his fuel, he'd lost track of him."

"And it took some time for the crew to get down to the water and get our boats going," Officer Vasquez said. "The police too."

Harriet could see more than a dozen boats, some heading out, some heading in, and they all looked the same to her.

"Keep your eyes out for O'Grady," Eli said.

"There are so many boats though," Harriet said. It was a gorgeous autumn Saturday. A perfect day on the water.

"There's ours," Officer Vasquez said, pointing to a group of boats racing out from the coast.

Now that she mentioned it, Harriet could see that they had the distinctive red and white paint of the Royal Coastguard. But she still didn't see Shane. Or know how she could tell which boat he was in. Harriet scanned the horizon while Eli steered the helicopter around, ducking down lower so they could see the boats better.

"Wait. Is that him?" Will asked, pointing at a boat. But that didn't make any sense. That boat was headed back to the marina.

"It looks like it could be, actually," Eli said.

"It's the same kind he has," Officer Vasquez said.

"But why is it going in?" Will asked.

"He's headed the wrong direction," Harriet said. "Annie and Paul wouldn't be going back to the marina."

But when Eli flew closer, it sure looked like Shane's boat to Harriet. It had the same color and shape, the same raised steering area.

"That's Shane," Will called. "I can see him driving."

Eli picked up the radio transmitter and spoke into it. "We have a visual on O'Grady. He's coming back to the marina. At your ten o'clock."

The Coastguard boats below them immediately turned toward Shane's boat. Two other boats—the police boat and Kyle's boat, Harriet was pretty sure, followed behind. It only took a few moments before Shane's boat was surrounded on all sides and he was forced to cut his motor.

Harriet and the others watched from the helicopter as someone on one of the Coastguard boats boarded Shane's boat and talked to him. It was hard to tell exactly what was going on, but it looked like the Coastguard officer was opening the cabin door, searching. A few minutes later, they heard a report over the radio. "It's just O'Grady. There's no one else on board."

"Where did they go?" Eli asked. "The others. Where are they?"

"Are you sure?" said a voice that Harriet recognized as DI McCormick.

"Very sure. There's nowhere for them to hide. They're not on this boat."

"Let's bring him in," DI McCormick said. "We have probable cause. He knows where they are."

"It feels somewhat anticlimactic, doesn't it?" Will said as Eli turned the helicopter back toward the base. "To not have found Annie and Paul after all?"

"We got O'Grady, at least," Eli said.

"Yeah, but he wasn't who we were looking for, is he?" Harriet said. "And Will and I don't think he knew what they were up to." She felt the same way Will did about not finding the Bellinghams. She'd really thought, after all this time, that they were going to find them and learn what really happened. They'd finally know what Annie and Paul had promised Shane to get his help and if she was right about what their plan had been. When Kyle reported that Shane had raced out of the marina, that he had Annie and Paul on board, she thought they'd finally get to question them.

The radio squawked again. "Calling all boats, this is HM Coastguard. We've just gotten a call from emergency services. Someone called to report that they were swept overboard in a storm and are floating on a life raft."

"A life raft?" Eli said.

Harriet saw Will's eyes widen, and his face registered the same shock she felt. It was them! It had to be!

"What is their location?" Eli asked into the radio.

"They don't know where they are," said the voice on the other end. "They say they've been lost at sea for several days. They say they finally got into an area with a signal and see a tall rock formation nearby. The call came in to Whitby emergency devices, though, so that's the general area. Any boat available to search the area, your help is requested."

"No way," Harriet said. "There's no way they've been out there this whole time and just got back into signal range. I don't believe that for a second."

"Of course that's not what happened," Will said. "Shane dropped them off, like they'd planned, but a few days later than expected."

"No wonder they weren't on his boat," Officer Vasquez said.

"Too bad 'a tall rock formation' could refer to any point along the coast," Eli said. "That doesn't narrow it down at all."

"But Shane can take them to where he dropped them off," Harriet said. She hoped with all her heart that Shane was an innocent party in all of this.

Someone asked over the radio whether the people were out there for real this time or if this was another hoax.

"Emergency services received a phone call from the couple," the first voice on the radio said. "We have no reason to believe this isn't real."

"If this is real, and if you guys are right, they're playing a very dangerous game," Eli said.

"But they can't be too far from here," Will said. "And Harriet's right. Shane can take them to the spot." He squeezed her hand reassuringly.

Eli banked the helicopter and turned back toward the open sea. "We should be able to spot them pretty easily if they're in close to the shore."

But when Harriet scanned the wide expanse below her, all she saw was water. Endless water, stretching all the way to the horizon. "And if he didn't drop them close to shore?"

"Then they could be anywhere."

"I see a lot of boats," Will said, peering down. "But no raft."

"It's bright orange," Officer Vasquez said. "We should be able to see it against the water."

"We should be able to," Eli said. "But I don't."

They had to be there somewhere. Shane wouldn't have gotten too far out into the bay before he dropped them off, not if he'd returned already. So where were they? Eli flew north, and then east, so they flew farther out over the sea. Below them, Harriet saw several boats headed out, as if to help search. Eli steered the helicopter up the coast and then back, but there was nothing that looked like a life raft.

Harriet began to get a sinking feeling in her stomach. "What if it really is a hoax again?" she asked. "What if they're not out there at all?"

"I have the opposite fear," Will said. "What if Shane dropped them off and we can't find them?"

"You mean, what if they actually do get swept out to sea?" Eli banked north again.

Will nodded. "That's exactly what I mean."

"Why can't we see them?" Harriet said. "Shouldn't we be able to see them?"

"It's like finding a needle in a haystack," Officer Vasquez said.

With the way the light reflected off the water, it was hard to see anything. Eli flew up and down the coast, slowly moving farther and farther away from shore while they searched the water. They were out far enough now that they flew over large tankers, enormous ships loaded with stacked shipping containers moving goods to London and Amsterdam and beyond. They were farther out than any of the search boats.

"Could they really be out this far, if Shane just dropped them off?" Harriet asked.

"The wind is pretty strong today," Officer Vasquez said. "If they caught the right current, sure they could."

Were they even down there? Were they truly adrift on the sea—but for real this time? The irony was not lost on Harriet that, in trying to stage their disappearance, they may very well have actually gotten themselves lost.

There was plenty of chatter over the radio, but no real news. Nothing to indicate the boats that searched for the missing raft had seen any sight of it. Harriet didn't know how long they were out there, flying up and down the coast. It was probably no more than an hour, but she'd lost all track of time.

"We're going to need to head back to base soon," Eli said after another eternity of fruitless minutes passed. "We're running low on petrol."

Now she was getting really worried. Could this ridiculous stunt actually end in tragedy? As much as she'd grown weary of Annie and Paul's tricks over the past week, and as much as she disliked what they'd done—to so many people—she didn't want them to die out there.

Please, Lord, help us find them. She heard Will softly humming the tune to "Eternal Father, Strong to Save."

Their efforts felt hopeless. But they were never truly without hope, Harriet reminded herself. The sea was dangerous, sure. It was rough and unpredictable and inhospitable. It could pull a person under so quickly and so deep that they'd never be found.

But even still, they didn't need to fear, because they knew the one who controlled the sea. The one who rebuked the storm with a word and walked on the surface of the water like it was solid ground.

God, even now, was in control.

Please, Lord, help us find them, she prayed again.

She blinked tears from her eyes and then blinked again.

Something caught her eye. Something that wouldn't dislodge as she blinked.

Wait. It wasn't something wrong with her eye. It was something on the water.

"Is that them?" Harriet pointed to the right, several hundred yards down the coast. It was just a speck, a tiny blip on the surface of the water. But she was pretty sure it was something.

"Is it?" Eli turned the copter and steered toward the speck, and as they got closer, it grew bigger.

"I think it might be," Officer Vasquez said excitedly.

"How did you see that?" Will asked.

"It's got to be them." As Eli piloted the helicopter closer and closer, Harriet could see that the speck was indeed a rubber raft, its bright orange color dulled by the reflection of the water. And on the raft, there were two people wearing life vests and waving their arms, frantically trying to signal to them.

Eli picked up the radio. "We found them."

CHAPTER TWENTY-THREE

The two Coastguard boats rushed to the location Eli gave them, and it wasn't long before Annie and Paul were headed back to the marina.

Harriet wasn't there when the couple was escorted off the boat, but she and Will were at the Coastguard station when the pair was brought there to be checked over by a medic before being turned over to the police.

"Thank you so much," Annie said as they were led inside. Her hair was greasy and matted, and she looked like she hadn't changed clothes in several days. Beside her, Paul had several days' worth of stubble, and his own clothes were soaked through. They looked nothing like the posh, well-groomed couple that appeared in their videos. "We floated for so long, we were sure we would never be found."

"We know you were only out there for a little over an hour," one of the officers—high up in the ranking, based on the bars on his uniform—said as the medic approached.

"We floated for days and days," Annie insisted, as if he hadn't just caught her in a lie.

"We survived by catching fish," Paul added. "And collecting rainwater in the bottom of our raft."

"You look remarkably well-fed if that's the case," the medic said.

So they were maintaining the farce that they'd been lost at sea, even though they all knew better. She wondered how long they would keep that up, and if they would ever admit what really happened.

"What about our dog? Did someone find our dog?" Annie asked. "We were so worried about her."

Now that Harriet knew they had deliberately left Mercedes on board by herself, she couldn't tamp down the anger she felt toward the culprits. "Mercedes is fine," she said through clenched teeth. "I'll see to it she goes to a good home."

Before they could react to her words, Annie and Paul were led into a room and the door closed behind them. Harriet supposed Shane was down at the police station. She and Will and Kyle hung around the Coastguard station for a while, hoping for news, but as the afternoon stretched into evening, it became increasingly clear they were in the way. Will suggested they head home, and Eli promised to let them know if he heard anything. Harriet was disappointed but tried not to show it.

It was just that she wanted to know what had really happened. If their guesses were right, and if this whole thing was a publicity stunt that had gone tremendously wrong. And, most important, if Shane was innocent of wrongdoing and hadn't gone back to his old ways.

Will took her hand as they walked toward the car, and Kyle walked next to them. Will was just opening the car door for Harriet when a police car drove into the lot. Harriet watched as an officer stepped out.

"Van!" Harriet tried not to seem too eager. "Is there any news?"

"We took O'Grady down to the police station. I'm here to give Eli and his team an update," Van said. "You might as well come in and hear it."

Will squeezed her hand, and Harriet tried not to show how excited she was. They followed him back into the station and were led into a conference room with a long table surrounded by chairs. Eli and Officer Vasquez were there, along with several other officers who Harriet assumed had been in boats on the water during the chase.

"Annie and Paul Bellingham will be transferred from this station to the police station to be questioned and will be placed under arrest," Van said. "The exact charges are still to be determined as we sort out what exactly happened but will include theft and fraud. The couple set things up to look like they'd been washed overboard in a storm, with the intention of filming footage and making a video for their social media channel."

Van dipped his chin at Harriet, and she nodded. If nothing else, she'd gotten that part right.

"But of course, they never intended to actually float in a life raft for very long. Their plan was to make it look like they'd been washed overboard, and then get picked up by another boat and hide out for a couple of days—just long enough to make sure their boat was discovered and their disappearance was noted."

"They'd hired O'Grady to ferry them back and forth?" Officer Vasquez asked.

"That's right," Van said. "He claims he wasn't aware of any of that. He showed us text messages in which the Bellinghams passed themselves off as Bethany Tucker and her brother, Clay. He says they told him their sailing companions were celebrating an anniversary the next day and asked if he could help them vacate the boat for two days to give the other couple privacy. They offered him a sizable fee, which he intended to use to repair his mother's kitchen."

"So he didn't realize he left the sailboat empty when he took Clay and Bethany—I mean, Paul and Annie—off?" Will asked.

"He didn't. He insists he would never have agreed to allow them on his boat if he'd known what they were really up to. He says he agreed to pick them up on Friday, let them stay on his boat, and be returned to the sailboat on Sunday."

Harriet frowned. But before she could get the question out, Van said, "You heard me right. We were under the assumption that the couple disappeared from the sailboat on Saturday night because it was found unmanned on Sunday after a storm the night before." He shook his head. "But texts between Shane and Paul show that Shane picked them up on *Friday* night."

"So that's another reason that Shane didn't know who they were!" Harriet said with profound relief. "There was no reason for him to connect siblings that he picked up on Friday with a married couple who disappeared on Saturday."

"And," Will added, "it stands to reason that the boat would have drifted so much in those two days, especially with the storm, that there was also no reason for him to think it was the same boat."

Harriet shook her head in amazement. "That means they put a fake entry in their logbook," she said. "Paul wrote about the storm as if they were in it. Actually, he wrote it before Saturday, and they were safe in Shane's boat at the marina the whole time."

"Shane had a special message for you, Harriet," Van said. "He wanted you to know he had no idea there was a dog on the boat. He was quite upset when we told him that."

"Even when I was worried he might be involved somehow, I never thought he would do something like that," Harriet said. "I'm glad to know I was right."

"So what went wrong?" Kyle asked. "Why didn't it go according to plan?"

"Shane's fuel line broke, or whatever it is fuel lines do," Harriet said. "Which meant they were stuck at the marina."

Will frowned. "They stayed in Shane's boat for days when they were supposed to be there one night," he said. "I wonder how they got away with that? Didn't Shane get suspicious that something was up?"

Van shook his head. "Annie faked illness or food poisoning or something, and Shane let them stay. They told him they'd pay him extra, but I don't know if he ever saw the money."

"But wait," one of the officers said. "Here's what I don't get. I know they weren't planning to be gone from their boat for very long. But even still, would they just let it go floating off without them? Surely they knew how dangerous that was, and how likely it was something would happen to the boat."

"What they said when we asked was that they felt sure the boat would be found and recovered before something bad happened. That, honestly, was integral to their plan, wasn't it? Someone had to find the empty boat and report it, which was how they'd get the huge number of views on their channel they were hoping for." Van shook his head, his feelings about their plan clear on his face.

"So what happened today? They just decided to go ahead with the whole farce, even though we were onto them?" Will asked. "And even though it was a week later, and no one could have possibly believed they'd survived lost at sea that long?"

"Not to mention that, even if they somehow survived that long in a rubber raft, they would have been found near Denmark, not just off the coast of Middlesborough," Eli said.

"Right," Van said. "Shane said they had him drop them off near Black Nab. That was the first he knew they had a life raft with them."

Harriet recognized the name of a rock formation off the coast in Saltwick Bay, south and east of Whitby. He hadn't taken them far at all then. She couldn't even imagine what the couple told him to persuade him to drop them off in a life raft in the open water.

"So how did they end up floating in the sea instead?" Will asked.

"It seems the currents were stronger than they realized," Van said. "They didn't make it to the rocks there before they were swept out to sea."

"So they really were in actual danger, just like they'd wanted to make it seem in their video," Eli said. "Talk about ironic."

"Luckily, tragedy was avoided," Van said. "But it could have gone another way, easily."

Harriet said a silent prayer of thanks for the Lord's protection. Annie and Paul were dishonest and presented a false view of their lives to the world, and in all likelihood would be found guilty of theft and fraud, among other things, but that didn't mean they were exempt from God's grace. They were still human beings, made in the image of God, and loved by their creator. Their lives were valuable, and she was grateful they'd been spared.

"Okay, but what if the sailboat hadn't been recovered in time?" Kyle asked. "What if it had been dashed against the rocks or capsized? What would they have done then?"

"Considering they never actually paid for the boat, I don't think they were as concerned about that as you'd think," Will said. "They wouldn't have been out any money, as it turns out."

"And it turns out they really didn't care about their dog," said Kyle angrily.

"We'll be asking about that and everything else, and digging into this more in the coming days," Van said. "There are still a lot of questions that need to be answered. What we can tell you right now is that it seems that Annie and Paul truly believed the boat would be recovered safely and returned to them, and that the video they planned to make from their misadventure would generate enough interest and income that it would be well worth all the expense and hassle."

"That's got to be a *lot* of money," Will said.

"I think they were making plenty," Van said. "For now, Harriet, do you mind caring for the dog a little longer? I suspect it will likely need a new home in the long run, but we'll have to wait to see how it all plays out."

"Of course." Harriet would have a hard time getting over her anger toward Annie and Paul, even if it turned out they thought Mercedes would be found before something happened to the boat. Anyone who could do that to a dog shouldn't be allowed to have one. She trusted things would be sorted out soon. For now, Mercedes had a good home.

"Even with all the money they hoped to make, they've got to be nuts," Kyle said, shaking his head. "Who in their right minds would think this sounded like a good plan?"

Harriet agreed with him, wholeheartedly. The world of influencers was one she didn't know much about and one she didn't plan to spend too much more time learning about.

They talked for a while longer, but Van couldn't answer many more questions about what had happened. He promised he would share more when he could. Harriet had a lot of questions about what would happen next, but for now, all the main things she hadn't understood had been addressed, so after Van left to head to the police station, Harriet took Will's hand and they walked together back out to the parking lot.

"That was quite an adventure," Will said as they drove home. The light began to fade from the sky, and a beautiful silver haze seemed to settle over the landscape. "How do you manage to get us involved in so many escapades?"

"I'd like to point out that I wasn't the one who got us involved in this one," Harriet said. "I never would have noticed that sailboat floating out there without anyone on board. That was all you."

Will laughed. "Maybe you're right about that."

"And you're the one who got us sent up in a helicopter today, by the way. That had nothing to do with me."

"It's a good thing I did."

"I don't disagree. Who knows what could have happened to Paul and Annie if we hadn't spotted them?"

"We have a lot to be thankful for," Will said.

They were mostly quiet the rest of the way home, each lost in their own thoughts, though Harriet could hear Will humming the Navy hymn under his breath.

When they walked in the door, Maxwell and Mercedes ran to greet them. Harriet petted them both and then collapsed on the sofa. They followed her across the room and sat at her feet. Will flopped down beside her, and Ash immediately jumped into his lap and started purring. Charlie hopped up on the back of the couch and added his motor to the mix.

"You did it," Will said, taking her hand. "Again."

"We all did it," Harriet said.

"Okay, but we really know that mostly you did it." He grinned at her.

"The important thing is they're safe." She didn't know what would happen to Annie and Paul, and she was relieved beyond telling that Shane had proved to be innocent of the whole affair. He might not have exercised the best judgment, but he hadn't intentionally done something shady. He wasn't the same person he once had been, and his life wasn't the same.

And neither was hers. She was so glad to be with Will, solving mysteries, figuring out the crazy adventure of marriage together.

For a moment, the only sound was the low growl of Ash and Charlie purring. There didn't seem to be anything more that needed to be said for now. Slowly, Harriet reached out her hand to Ash. Instead of hissing at her, the little cat moved his head forward and sniffed at her fingers. When he didn't pull back, she gently stroked his head.

"Look at that," Will said. "See? I knew it wouldn't take much longer."

Ash was still purring. He seemed hesitant but let her stroke his head. "I'll win him over yet."

For now she was content to bask in the glow of a small victory.

"So, since that adventure is behind us," Will said after a few minutes, "are you ready for another one?"

"Another one?" Harriet laughed. "We don't even get a few hours' break between adventures?"

"We won't be leaving for a few months, but we would need to start planning now."

"Leaving?" Harriet said. "Where are we going?"

"Scotland," Will said. "I thought that it's time we get you to Muckle Roe. My dad is excited about the idea of you coming to visit. Would you like to go?"

"Are you kidding?" Harriet's heart swelled at the idea. "I would love that. I would absolutely love to see where you're from."

"Oh good," Will said. "Because I found an insane deal I couldn't pass up and I bought plane tickets today."

"You what?" Harriet said with a delighted laugh.

"They're refundable for twenty-four hours. But I figured you weren't going to say no. There's no place on earth more beautiful than Scotland. Why wouldn't you want to go?"

She laughed again. She supposed everyone felt like that about the place they were from. Home was always the best place in the world.

"When are we going?"

"In a couple of months."

"I'm excited." Harriet leaned forward and kissed him. "I can't wait to see your home."

"Scotland is just the place I'm from," Will said, pressing his forehead against hers. "Home is wherever you are."

Harriet smiled and settled back on the couch. Home, for her, was Will. It was being in his life. Merging their lives together. Two becoming one.

"Look," Will said, as Ash slowly pushed himself up and walked over to Harriet. She held her breath while he sniffed her, and then, tentatively, put one paw on her leg. She stroked his back as he stepped into her lap. "I knew he'd learn to love you. It just took a little time."

Harriet continued to stroke the kitten, and he purred and used his paws to knead her legs. Harriet rubbed his ears and thought, *If Ash can make adjustments for this new life, so can I.*

There would be ups and downs as she and Will got used to living with each other, but with God's help and grace, they would face this life—with whatever adventures came their way—together.

FROM THE AUTHOR

Dear Reader,

I was lucky enough to visit Yorkshire and to see Robin Hood's Bay, the real town our fictional village is based on, earlier this year, and I was so excited to get to visit it again in the pages of this book. As I tried to think of an interesting mystery to write about, I looked back through my photos from the trip, and I found a photo of a strange red object I'd taken a picture of for some reason. Actually, I know the reason—it was because it was so quirky. It was a big round orb, painted bright red, with the words SHIPWRECKED MARINER'S SOCIETY painted on it in black. I had no clue what it was or what it meant, but I thought it was so peculiar and so British, that I snapped a photo and promptly forgot about it. (Sadly, I didn't snap a photo of the RNLI Collecting Cod or the *Visiter* plaque, both of which are real and mentioned in this story.)

After I found the photo, I looked up the Shipwrecked Mariner's Society and discovered that the red thing I'd seen was a World War II mine, and that it was now used as a collection point for donations for the charity, which, as its name suggests, has long helped boaters in need. It's a worthy organization with a long and storied history. After seeing the photo, I became interested in the idea of shipwrecks along this part of the coast, and the idea for a boat-based mystery was born.

There were a lot of different directions I wanted to take the story—including having Harriet research old shipwrecks in the area—but I couldn't shake the image of a sailboat rolling along in the waves with no one on board. So Annie and Paul and their vanishing act were born. But I also made sure to include a subplot about the most famous shipwreck on the Yorkshire coast.

As much as I enjoyed researching and writing about what it would be like to live on a sailboat—something I will surely never have the chance to do, but one can dream, right?—my favorite part of this story was writing about Harriet and Will as they try to figure out how to live together in the early days of their marriage. I've now been married for nearly twenty years, but the joys and struggles of those early days are still fresh. I loved my new husband more than I ever imagined possible. But that didn't always make it easy to live with him, and he would no doubt say the same thing about me. Merging two lives and learning about each other's rhythms, preferences, and needs was challenging, but we got through it, and here we are all these years later. (And after that first time, my husband never again asked a friend home for dinner without consulting me!)

I hope you enjoyed this story as much as I enjoyed writing it.

Beth Adams

ABOUT THE AUTHOR

Beth Adams lives in Brooklyn, New York, with her husband and two daughters. When she's not writing, she's trying to find time to read mysteries.

A STROLL THROUGH THE ENGLISH COUNTRYSIDE

The Wreck of the *Visiter*

The shipwreck of the *Visiter* is a true story, though I took the liberty of changing its location to our village of White Church Bay for this book. On January 16, 1881, the brigantine *Visiter*, sailing from Newcastle to London, faced ice and strong winds and broke apart just south of Robin Hood's Bay. The six sailors on board made it to the ship's lifeboat and clung to it overnight as the storm raged.

In the morning, they were spotted from Robin Hood's Bay, but the town's lifeboat—you can still see a replica of an old lifeboat on the spillway in town—was deemed not up to the conditions. The vicar in Robin Hood's Bay sent a message to the larger town of Whitby, but the conditions were too rough for their lifeboat to launch from that port, so it truly was carried over the road, through snow and ice, the six miles to Robin Hood's Bay. Incredibly, they made it, and the lifeboat was launched from the spillway, but that first attempt failed, as the raging sea snapped several oars. A second attempt was made, and the lifeboat successfully rescued all the sailors.

The *Visiter* was registered in Whitby to a Trueman Robinson, but everything else I've written about Trueman is completely made up. I have no reason to suspect there was anything but coal on board the boat when it went down (though Robin Hood's Bay actually was known as a smuggler's haven, so who knows?) and there is no record of a tortoise on board, at least as far as I know.

However, it is true that the Seychelles giant tortoise can live for at least one hundred and ninety years (look up Jonathan!), so if there had been one on board that ship that managed to survive, it is entirely possible it would still be around today.

YORKSHIRE YUMMIES

Harriet's Cacio e Pepe

You can find this pasta dish all over Rome, and it's so delicious and not at all hard to make. It's easy to pull together quickly when your husband brings home guests without advance warning!

Ingredients:

- 1½ cups finely grated Pecorino Romano
- 1 cup finely grated Parmigiano-Reggiano
- 1 tablespoon freshly ground black pepper
- ¾ pound long pasta, like spaghetti or fettucine
- olive oil

Directions:
Put a big pot of water on to boil, and salt it well. Combine cheeses and fresh ground pepper in large bowl and sprinkle with a few drops of water. You want to add just enough water to be able to stir it into a thick paste.

Cook pasta in boiling water. Reserve a cup of pasta water and then use tongs to transfer pasta to the bowl. Stir vigorously to coat pasta in the cheesy watery paste. It will look like a mess at first, but stick with it, and stir really well. If you need to thin the sauce, add a drop or two of olive oil and a few drops of pasta water. The sauce should end up creamy but not watery.

Dust with additional cheese or more pepper if desired and serve.

Read on for a sneak peek of another exciting book in the Mysteries of Cobble Hill Farm *series!*

Pride, Prejudice, and Pitfalls

BY JOHNNIE ALEXANDER

Harriet Bailey—now Harriet Bailey-Knight—listened intently as Garth Hamblin, playing the part of George Wickham, confided the injustices done to him after the death of his nemesis's father. They were seated next to each other on two straight-backed chairs, which were uncomfortable substitutes for a Victorian settee. Other residents of the White Church Bay community played quiet games of whist at two nearby card tables while those standing by the faux fireplace engaged in muted conversations.

"I do not wish to speak ill of the son," Garth said to Harriet, "despite his abominable treatment toward me. Though I can assure you that he will not hinder my enjoyment of such pleasant company as this evening has afforded. Should he be present at such gatherings, my behavior shall be in keeping with the decorum required by polite society. His elevated status will not keep me away."

"I'm glad to hear it." Harriet formed her lips into a smile that— she hoped—exuded Elizabeth Bennet's ladylike interest in George

Wickham. Multiple times, she'd admitted that this acting business was more complicated than she'd expected.

At least this scene between Jane Austen's famed *Pride and Prejudice* protagonist and the charming son of the Pemberley estate's former steward wasn't too difficult to portray. Harriet genuinely liked Garth, a wildlife rehabilitation specialist for the nearby Yorkshire Coast Wildlife Centre. Their professional relationship had deepened into friendship a few months ago when they teamed up to find a rare pine marten that needed veterinary care.

The scenes that came later, after Elizabeth learns of Wickham's true nature, required Harriet to dig deeper into her limited acting repertoire. Showing polite scorn to Garth wasn't her major acting challenge, however. That came from pretending she felt nothing but contempt for the handsome Fitzwilliam Darcy.

In this amateur production, the role of Darcy, Pemberley's owner, was played by the handsome Fitzwilliam "Will" Knight.

The same man Harriet had married, in real life, only a couple of months before.

As Garth recited his next line, Lydia Bennet interrupted Elizabeth and Wickham's tête-à-tête. After delivering her sassy lines, Elena Hazeldine dragged Garth to downstage center, where other couples took their places for a lively jig.

As the lighting over the straight-backed chairs dimmed, Harriet relaxed and focused her gaze on Elena and Garth. Those two didn't need to feign their attraction, not when Elena practically glowed and Garth could barely take his eyes off her during the dance. The young widower, alone for several years, had shown no interest in giving away his heart again...until he'd met Elena. Now they were an official couple, with Jack, Elena's seven-year-old orphaned nephew, a very welcome third wheel.

Lost in her thoughts, Harriet startled when a woman plopped onto the chair beside her.

"I'm so glad I found you here." Poppy Schofield's stage whisper seemed to bounce to the front of the stage and back again.

Harriet placed her index finger against her lips. "We're rehearsing," she whispered.

Poppy's features scrunched together as she pointed to the dancers. "*They're* rehearsing. We're chatting in the corner like the two wallflowers we are. It's no different than if we were at the home of Mr. and Mrs. Phillips. Spectators instead of participants."

She breathed out a lingering sigh and rested her interlaced fingers on her tweed skirt. "Two unattached women longing for our knights in shining armor to give us our fairy-tale ending."

Harriet had barely squelched her amusement at Poppy's unexpected shift from scolding schoolmarm to dreamy romantic when a sharp elbow jabbed her in the ribs. "Though you already got your Knight, didn't you?"

"That I did," Harriet whispered as if she hadn't heard similar jokes a gazillion times in the past few months. She'd never tire of them, and she could already imagine relaying this conversation to Will later tonight. That was, if neither of them were called to any after-hours emergencies. Such was the life of a veterinarian married to a pastor.

A life they embraced, considering it a small price to pay for living it together.

Though they both wondered why their veterinary or pastoral emergencies couldn't happen on the same evenings instead of calling only one or the other away from home.

"It's such a blessing to have Pastor Will all married and settled. But I have to say I'm surprised you didn't sign up for any of the church's autumn bazaar committees." Poppy spoke without a hint of reproach, but the words stabbed Harriet all the same.

"Besides, everyone will expect to see you helping out," Poppy continued, "you being the pastor's wife and all. As much as we all love and appreciate Pastor Will, there's been a kind of emptiness in the church since Reverend Cummings left. Janice Cummings was such an energetic pastor's wife. It was often said she spent more time at the church than her husband did."

Harriet inwardly winced as Poppy's stage whisper increased in volume. She gestured to the nearby wing then stood and headed that way. Thankfully, Poppy followed.

Once she'd positioned herself so she could keep an eye on the play's director, who had the actors rehearsing the dance again, Harriet gave Poppy an apologetic smile. "Will and I already talked about my involvement with the bazaar. Because this is a busy time of year for the clinic, we decided I could help whenever I was free instead of signing up for a committee."

Poppy's lips turned downward as she appeared to process this strange idea. Perhaps strange to her mind, but Harriet thought it wise. It was October, and tupping season, the time when farmers put their rams and ewes together, was coming soon. Between now and then, Harriet needed to examine the farmers' stock to be sure they were in top condition for breeding and lambing. Those farm visits needed to be scheduled around her routine clinic appointments.

Before Poppy could respond, Harriet rushed on. "Aunt Jinny is on the banquet decorations committee, and Polly is in charge of the children's games. They both agreed I could pop in and out of their committee meetings as my time allowed. I already promised Aunt Jinny I would help with the table centerpieces in my free time."

Though any free time seemed to be a pipe dream at the moment.

"Jinny isn't even here," Poppy said. "Though I guess I shouldn't begrudge her an opportunity to visit Vienna."

Harriet's aunt had joined her son, a pharmacist who was attending a professional conference, and his wife, on the trip while his mother-in-law stayed with their seven-year-old twins. "She's having a great time sightseeing with Olivia. Anthony has been able to join them when his schedule allows. Besides, knowing Aunt Jinny, she already has a folder filled with decorating ideas for the banquet."

"The timing could have been better though."

"She didn't pick the dates for the conference," Harriet protested.

"I know that," Poppy replied with a girlish giggle. "It is what it is. Just like this play. Everyone is more interested in it than in making sure the bazaar is a success."

Harriet wasn't sure about that. Only about half of the people involved with the play attended White Church. The other half might attend the bazaar, but that would be their only involvement.

"That seems upside down to me, as if the bazaar isn't worth sacrificing something else for," Poppy continued. "Everyone claims to be so busy, but I'm busy too. You have no idea how early I get up to start my baking each morning, and yet I'm finding the time to supervise the entire bazaar."

Considering that the Biscuit Bistro, Poppy's adorable cookie shop located in White Church Bay's historic area, never opened before ten, Harriet had her doubts that Poppy's alarm was set much earlier than Harriet's own. Especially this time of year, when tourists were few and the shop opened for only a few hours a day during the week and closed on Sundays.

"Besides, being overworked or tired isn't an excuse when we're called to do the Lord's work." Poppy being Poppy, the rebuke was wrapped in cheer, as if it were one of her signature icing-covered shortbreads. "No one should know that better than the pastor's wife."

"I'm still a novice at being a pastor's wife." Surely even the incomparable Janice Cummings needed time—and the congregation's grace—before she became the embodiment of all the best qualities of the role.

"All I'm saying," Poppy replied, "is that using the clinic as an excuse seems especially odd when you've taken on one of the major roles in this play. Some people might wonder how you have time for rehearsals but no time to volunteer for the bazaar."

"Simple," Harriet said, even though there was more to her answer than she intended to share with Poppy. "I agreed to be in the play weeks before the autumn bazaar board held their first organizational meeting."

"But you were here last year. You must have known the bazaar is an annual event and in need of a multitude of hands."

Harriet swallowed a defeated sigh. Last year, she'd donated a trio of Cobble Hill Vet Clinic gift certificates for the banquet's silent auction and helped Will organize the teen talent show. No one had expected anything more from her than that. In fact, her small contributions to the event had been gushed over.

The congregation's expectations certainly had changed since she and Will exchanged their "I do's." At least five or six times in the past two months, someone had informed her about how Janice Cummings had done this or that.

"You should have seen the floral arrangements that Janice created for the vestibule. They were breathtaking."

"Was there anyone who could organize the volunteer appreciation dinner better than Janice?"

"No one ever worked harder than Janice on Spruce Up the Church Day."

No matter how often Will told Harriet not to take the not-quite-so-veiled criticisms to heart, she couldn't help feeling she wasn't measuring up in the eyes of her husband's congregants. Maybe she should officially join at least one committee, although she didn't know how she'd fit regular meetings into her already crowded schedule.

She'd even considered dropping out of the play. But Will had been adamant—if she wasn't Elizabeth, he wouldn't be Darcy. And they simply couldn't do that to Joel, Will's old friend. Though, perhaps, "former acquaintance" was a more apt description of their relationship. Joel Elphick, the director and new owner of the Beacon-on-the-Moor Playhouse, needed all the help he could get if his first production was to be a success.

The dance music faded, and Joel's voice resounded from the fourth row of theater seats. "Great job, everyone."

The auditorium lights came on over that section as he stood and flung out both arms as if to invite the entire cast into a virtual hug. He held a sheaf of papers attached to a clipboard in one hand, and the infamous red pen he used to scrawl his notes on each actor's performance in the other.

His neatly trimmed beard added maturity to his otherwise boyish features. However, these were accentuated by the crimson and gold soccer club ball cap hiding his prematurely receding hairline. Though no expert on male fashion, Harriet sensed Joel couldn't make up his mind about the persona he wanted to project to the world—that of the sophisticated artist or one of youthful exuberance.

Even his clothing, a tidy knitted sweater over a casual untucked shirt, seemed to send a mixed message. Or perhaps she was letting the little she knew of Joel's past unfairly influence her impression of him.

As Joel moved toward the front of the stage, Harriet touched the sleeve of Poppy's cardigan. "You'll have to excuse me. I need to hear what he has to say."

She joined the other actors gathering near the footlights, but apparently Poppy didn't intend to be dismissed so easily. Though she didn't have a role in the play, she scurried along behind Harriet.

"This is so exciting," she gushed. "A theater of our own being brought back to life again before our very eyes. My grandmother used to tell me stories of coming here when she was a girl. And every December she brought my mother to see *The Nutcracker*."

Poppy's excitement mellowed into wistfulness. "It was their holiday tradition. One Mother wished to share with me, but the Playhouse closed before I was old enough to sit through a ballet."

The amateur actress playing Mary Bennet, an older teen with round spectacles and brown hair pulled into a severe bun at the nape of her neck, glared at Poppy and Harriet.

"Do you mind?" she snarled before turning her back on them.

Red blotches colored Poppy's pale cheeks as she pressed her lips together. Harriet grimaced, regretting she hadn't somehow stopped Poppy's patter before "Mary" embarrassed her. On the flip side, at least now she could focus on what Joel was saying to the cast.

After a few constructive critiques to specific individuals, he stepped back with a wide smile. "We'll go through the scene one more time and then move on to the next one. Before you take your places, however, I want to say a special thank-you to a delightful woman who blesses all of us with her generosity and biscuit-baking skills. Several times a week, Poppy Schofield brings us treats from her shop without asking anything in return. Let's show her how much we appreciate her!"

Joel tucked the clipboard beneath his arm and clapped while a pleasant pink flush replaced the red blotchiness on Poppy's cheeks. Harriet pulled her into a side hug as the cast members clapped along with the director. Even "Mary" joined in, though without any enthusiasm.

When a few others approached Poppy to share a hug or express their personal thanks, Harriet moved out of the way. Joel caught her eye and winked, as if to answer her silent question. She nodded, certain now her suspicion that he'd overheard "Mary's" impolite reprimand was correct.

True, Poppy's incessant talking was impolite too. But only one of the two had been unkind. And that individual didn't share a name with a petite red flower.

As Harriet returned to the straight-backed chairs pretending to be a settee, she glanced at her watch. Once she-as-Elizabeth finished her brief conversation with Garth-as-Wickham, she would make a discreet exit and return to the clinic. Joel shouldn't mind, since she wasn't needed for the dance or for the next scene scheduled for rehearsal.

If neither she nor Garth flubbed their lines, she might have time to stop in at the church before heading to the clinic for her late-afternoon appointments. If Will had a few minutes, she'd tell him about Joel's charitable behavior toward Poppy. Even such a small interaction might help alleviate her husband's doubts about his friend's character. And reassure him that he was right to give Joel a second chance.

Harriet was about to take her seat when a bloodcurdling scream silenced all conversation and glued the actors' feet to the boards. A moment later, Kezia Ellsworth emerged from the stage-left curtains and stumbled toward Harriet.

The rail-thin woman practically collapsed before Harriet could grip her elbows and hold her steady. Her blue eyes, wide open and cold with fear, stared at Harriet.

"I—I saw—" Kezia stammered as tears streamed down her bloodless cheeks. "I saw a ghost."

A NOTE FROM THE EDITORS

We hope you enjoyed another exciting volume in the Mysteries of Cobble Hill Farm series, published by Guideposts. For over seventy-five years, Guideposts, a nonprofit organization, has been driven by a vision of a world filled with hope. We aspire to be the voice of a trusted friend, a friend who makes you feel more hopeful and connected.

By making a purchase from Guideposts, you join our community in touching millions of lives, inspiring them to believe that all things are possible through faith, hope, and prayer. Your continued support allows us to provide uplifting resources to those in need. Whether through our communities, websites, apps, or publications, we inspire our audiences, bring them together, and comfort, uplift, entertain, and guide them. Visit us at guideposts.org to learn more.

We would love to hear from you. Write us at Guideposts, P.O. Box 5815, Harlan, Iowa 51593 or call us at (800) 932-2145. Did you love *Lost at Sea*? Leave a review for this product on guideposts.org/shop. Your feedback helps others in our community find relevant products.

Find inspiration, find faith, find Guideposts.
Shop our best sellers and favorites at
guideposts.org/shop

Or scan the QR code to go directly to our Shop.